Biblical Multicultural Teams

Biblical Multicultural Teams

Applying Biblical Truth to *Cultural Differences*

Sheryl Takagi Silzer

WILLIAM CAREY INTERNATIONAL UNIVERSITY PRESS
PASADENA, CALIFORNIA

William Carey International University Press

1539 E. Howard St.
Pasadena, California 91104
Email: wciupress_orders@wciu.edu

Cover Design: Renee Robitaille

Sheryl Takagi Silzer, Author
Biblical Multicultural Teams:
Applying Biblical Truth to Cultural Differences

ISBN: 9780865850156

Library of Congress Identification Number: 2011930652

Dedicated

To fellow Christian workers who struggle with cross-cultural misunderstandings on a daily basis yet have a deep desire to present the transforming message of the Gospel to the peoples of the world

CONTENTS

CHAPTER FOUR

CHAPTER FIVE

CHAPTER SIX

CHAPTER SEVEN

CHAPTER EIGHT

CHAPTER NINE

CHAPTER TEN

ACKNOWLEDGEMENTS

This book documents my journey of cultural self-discovery that began after twenty-five years of on-going cross-cultural stress. Only by God's grace and mercy have I been able to begin this journey. I also want to thank the numerous people who have encouraged and helped me along the way.

First of all, I want to thank Sherwood Lingenfelter, who introduced me to Mary Douglas' theory of culture, and both Sherwood and Judith Lingenfelter, whose courses helped me process my cultural stress.

Judith Lingenfelter and Marguerite Kraft encouraged me to use my experience in the Women in Mission course, which I taught for the first time in 1993. My students graciously worked through the first draft of the material and made valuable suggestions.

I also want to thank Dan Shaw, my doctoral advisor, for his encouragement through my dissertation process and for his on-going interest in the development and use of these materials in workshops around the world.

I am very grateful for my students at Biola University and for the many workshop participants from SIL International and partner organizations. By sharing examples from their personal lives and ministry they have helped improve the contents of the book.

I also want to thank my sister-in-law, Masako Takagi, and others who patiently read through numerous drafts. Most of all I want to thank my husband, who endured much of my cross-cultural stress yet patiently loved me along my journey of self discovery. He has also been my primary editor and has helped me through innumerable drafts. Without his help and encouragement this book could not have made it this far.

Foreword

During my years on the faculty at Biola University, Sheryl and Pete Silzer were colleagues, assigned to Biola by SIL International. During that time Sheryl participated in one of my seminars on anthropological theory, and we explored together the theoretical importance of cultural definitions of space, and the social relationships that occur in the common spaces of household and work. Coming from a Japanese cultural heritage, where culturally defined spaces played a critical role in her life and worldview, Sheryl grasped quickly how culture expressed in space has profound affect on how people see and understand their social worlds. She went on to complete her PhD, wrestling with the issues of how Christians, who are always people of and within culture, can fulfill their purpose and calling as people created in the image of God, and servants of their Lord Jesus Christ.

In this work Dr. Silzer provides a fresh examination of how cultural definitions of space and relationships within space produce our "Culture-based Judging System." By exploring cultural variations in household space, and the basic human activities of visiting, eating, working, resting, and cleaning within those spaces, she helps the reader understand how we become accustomed to familiar ways, and how those ways ground us in our "Culture-based Judging System."

This book is profoundly practical, written for men and women who seek to follow the call of God to minister in multicultural partnerships for the mission of God through the global church. Silzer connects us to the culture that governs our daily habits of life, and shines light into the darkness of how those habits become the basis for judgment and condemnation of others, particularly when we try to work outside of our comfortable cultural frames. She then illuminates how our cultural biases (as seen through variation in values for structure and community) frame the fundamental aspects of cultural life. As a long time student of culture and author regarding the challenges of culture and mission, I have found this book original and a very helpful contribution to the challenges of living and working together in multicultural teams. Because Silzer connects us to the ordinary aspects of our cultural life, we cannot ignore either our biases, or our propensity to judge and condemn others out of those biases. Most importantly, she helps the reader think much more deeply about what it means to be a cultural person made in the image of God, and called to live in loving relationships to one another in multicultural contexts.

Sherwood Lingenfelter
Fuller Theological Seminary
May 26, 2011

INTRODUCTION

ABOUT THE AUTHOR

My name tells you a lot about me: Sheryl Takagi Silzer. I grew up with my Takagi family in Southern California, but was surrounded by non-Japanese. My parents chose my first name as a way to help me "melt" into the great American melting pot of cultures rather than identify with my Japanese heritage. As a third generation Japanese American, I've interacted multiculturally all my life. I married a German/British/Irish American and have related to my Silzer relatives for almost 40 years. I have also been a part of a multinational mission organization serving in North and South America, Asia, and the Pacific for over 40 years. Therefore, this book has grown out of a need to better understand culture, both my own and the cultures with which I have worked over the years.

UNDERSTANDING CULTURE

Working with or relating to people from other cultural backgrounds, whether in the global workplace or in day-to-day social interactions, is the norm in the twenty-first century. These multicultural interactions inherently have many cross-cultural misunderstandings, but are seldom understood or addressed appropriately. As a result, various negative emotions—frustration, disappointment, anxiety, fear, upset feelings, and anger—grow over time and compound the misunderstandings. Unfortunately, most people do not understand that many of these misunderstandings could easily be cleared up with a better understanding of our own culture or what Lingenfelter calls our "default culture" is. That is, the way we learned to do things in our childhood home (Lingenfelter 2008, 71).[1]

When we encounter different ways of doing things in our adult life, we often respond to differences in the same way our parents modeled when we were nurtured or disciplined as a child. That is, if our parents got upset, frustrated, or angry when we didn't do as they instructed, in our adult life we will likely get upset, frustrated, or angry when others do things differently than we do. We have a built-in system that maintains our way of doing things. This is a "Culture-based Judging System" (CbJS) that reveals what we think is right and wrong (Hiebert 2009a, 379).[2]

The degree to which we react negatively to differences typically arises from how we were nurtured and disciplined growing up. We were nurtured and disciplined according to a cultural way of doing things, and our identity became associated with that ideal. How our parents or caretakers nurtured and disciplined us shapes how we respond to cultural differences today. If we did something that our parents did not want us to do, they might have responded with upset feelings, anger, or sadness. Very few parents stop to examine why their children do the things they do; they merely react in culturally appropriate ways. In mostly unconscious ways, our individual and collective histories of how people have treated us impact our present day multicultural relationships. Rather than accepting people's actions as a normal result of cultural differences, we normally interpret them as being specifically against our way of doing things. Because we have done things in the same way for so long, we actually believe our way is the biblical way, implying the other ways are wrong (Dye 2009, 469-473).[3] Therefore, we feel justified in expressing negative emotions and acting wrongly towards people who don't agree with us.

> As Christians, we are often unaware that our beliefs are frequently shaped more by our culture than the gospel. We take our Christianity to be biblically based and normative for everyone. We do not stop to ask what parts of it come from our sociocultural and historical contexts, and what parts come form Scripture. (Hiebert 2009b,18)

Even though we know Christ commands us to forgive one another (Matthew 6:14) and to be reconciled to God and to one another (2 Corinthians 5:18), we are unable to extend God's grace to others because we misinterpret their intentions and hold false beliefs about ourselves. The cultural false belief we have is a mistaken view of who we are as made in the image of God, and this false belief prevents us from accepting others as made in God's image.

Multicultural interaction requires understanding why others do things differently and why their way of doing things bothers or offends us. Learning how the Culture-based Judging System of our cultural type works will help us understand ourselves as well as others. It will also enable us to begin the process of replacing the habits of our cultural type with biblical truth. With God's help we will then be able to be fully reconciled to God in cultural interaction with others and join Him as a minister of reconciliation bringing God's shalom to ourselves and to others.

Mary Douglas, a British social anthropologist, in her description of cultural types, describes how a preference or "cultural bias" for one cultural type rejects the other cultural types in order to reinforce the preferred type. This bias is maintained through our "Culture-based Judging System" (CbJS). Our CbJS is based on a set of beliefs that reacts negatively to other ways of doing things. We use various negative responses (words and/or actions) to justify our cultural preferences (Douglas 1992, 6, 1982).

PERSONAL REFLECTION ON CULTURAL TYPE

For most of my life I did not understand what my cultural type was or why my Culture-based Judging System caused me so much cross-cultural stress. It wasn't until I went back to school after many years of living overseas and studied culture that I began to realize how much my cultural upbringing (both Asian and American) influenced me and produced so much cross-cultural stress. When I started looking back at my childhood and learned how my cultural type was first formed, I began to understand how it created preferences that "Culture-based Judging System."[4]

When we encounter cultural differences, our CbJS kicks in. Because I unconsciously held strongly to my cultural type, I decided that the cultural differences I faced overseas were wrong (and my way was right). I justified my negative responses to other cultural patterns—frustration, anxiety, fear, anger, complaining about other cultures, avoiding, or projecting my negative emotions on them. Although I knew that my thoughts and actions did not measure up to God's standard for my behavior, I still tended to respond in these negative ways to cultural differences.

CULTURAL TYPE VS. BIBLICAL TRUTH

Although our negative responses to other cultures do not align with biblical truth, Christians often mistakenly think our cultural type represents biblical truth. By saying our cultural preferences are biblical we distort God's truth.

Samuel Escobar highlights the importance of understanding the difference between our culture and biblical teaching in an article about mission trends:

> One of the evangelical missiological trends after Lausanne 1974 posed forcefully the need for evangelists and missionaries to become aware of how their culture shaped not only their missionary methodologies, but also their versions of the gospel, in ways that were in open contrast with biblical teaching and theological conviction (Escobar 2003,5).

When I reflected on my cross-cultural experiences I began to understand that my cultural beliefs about myself were very different from God's view of me as being created in His image. My actions did not reflect the truth that God loves me for who I am, not for what I do. I had thought God only loved me if I was busy doing various Christian activities.

My cultural type created beliefs about myself that were not aligned with God's truth. My automatic CbJS justified these beliefs so that the natural response was stress, frustration, anxiety, fear, anger, and negative actions. When God began to show me the false beliefs of my cultural type, He also helped me believe His truth. As a result, my negative emotions and actions were replaced with His love, joy, peace, and other fruit of the Spirit. The change in my belief about myself also changed my attitude towards others. I began to see them as God saw me. My perspective of my multicultural teammates began to change when I understood how the CbJS of my cultural type distorted the image of God in me through my decision making, my beliefs, and my emotional responses to cultural differences.

Applying Truth to Cultural Differences

The main purpose of this book is to foster biblical multicultural teams by helping them to recognize how their Culture-based Judging System works and apply biblical truth to cultural differences. As you read this book you will learn what it means to be made in the image of God (Chapter 1). You will also discover how the CbJS of your cultural type distorts the image of God (Chapters 2-9). In the final chapter you will learn how to apply biblical truth to cultural differences so that individuals from different cultures can thrive and flourish in biblical multicultural teams (Chapter 10).

This book will guide you through a series of topics and exercises about the cultural practices in your childhood home. As you revisit various areas of your upbringing you will examine how your CbJS was formed and how it continues to influence you today. Five essential topics will show you how the CbJS of your cultural type replaces biblical truth:

1. What it means to be created in the image of God. (Chapter 1)
2. How your CbJS works. (Chapter 2)
3. How your childhood family shapes your CbJS. (Chapter 3)
4. How your childhood home shapes your CbJS. (Chapter 4)
5. How your childhood cultural practices (visiting, eating, working, resting, cleaning) shape your CbJS. (Chapter 5-9)

The final goal of this book is to suggest ways you can apply biblical truth to your CbJS (Chapter 10).

Although the ideal presented in this book is a "Biblical Multicultural Team," the reality is that a "biblical" multicultural team is very difficult to achieve this side of heaven. On the other hand, unless we intentionally choose to be "biblical," our mission organizations, Christian churches, Christian schools, and other Christian groups will continue to be characterized by on-going misunderstandings, conflicts, and unresolved cultural issues. Without God's help we will not demonstrate what it means to be made in the image of God.

In order to understand the major concepts in the book and the ideal of biblical multicultural teams, you will need to understand the following key terms:

1. Biblical Truth—what God says about who He is and who we are as created in His image (will, mind, and heart). That is, whether our decision making is based on God's truth, guided by His Spirit, and demonstrated in our relationships with God and others.

2. Biblical Multicultural Teams—multicultural teams that understand how their CbJSs distort the image of God and that are replacing their cultural type with biblical truth. Individuals from different cultures on these teams are thriving and flourishing in this process.

3. Culture—everyday way of doing things such as interacting with family members and visiting, eating, working, resting, and cleaning activities.

4. Culture-based Judging System—the mechanism people use to maintain their cultural type by validating their way of doing things by "judging" others' ways of speech, thought, actions, behavior, as wrong/bad/less valuable.

5. Cultural Type—our preferred way of doing things, one of the four types of cultures described by Mary Douglas (See Chapter 2). Our cultural type is shaped primarily by patterns learned in our childhood home.

This book uses two simple tools to help you recognize and understand the CbJS of your cultural type—a family tree and a house floor plan of your childhood home.[5]

Drawing your family tree will help you discuss and compare your family with others (particularly people from other cultural backgrounds). Your family tree describes the structure of your family—the number of people (parents, siblings, others), the percentage of males and females, birth order, particular characteristics of your family, and present day family relationships. Sharing this information with others can lead to a greater awareness of yourself and other members of your team.

Drawing the house floor plan of the house where you grew up will help you remember childhood experiences. Comparing your home with those of others on your team will reveal cultural differences or affirm cultural similarities. The house floor plan also provides a guide to jog your memory as you revisit the childhood cultural practices of visiting, eating, working, resting, and cleaning.

These two tools are not an end in themselves, but when you use them to share your childhood experiences, they will raise your cultural self-awareness and increase the bond you have with others.

This book is based on six assumptions:

1. People are shaped by their childhood upbringing, as well as their language, culture, socialization, religion, history, economy, and personal experiences. This book focuses primarily on the impact of cultural preferences formed in childhood because they have been shown to influence present-day multicultural relationships.

2. Due to globalization, immigration, and other factors, it is difficult to describe a particular culture as a unified whole. The cultural descriptions in this book, taken from many different sources, are intended to help you discover your own cultural type and how its inherent CbJS replaces biblical truth. The descriptions of particular cultures should not be used as stereotypes or to validate your CbJS.

3. Every person and every culture reflects something of the image of God. Therefore, we can learn something about God from each person and each culture. The focus of this statement is to emphasize God's desire for greater multicultural interaction to help you learn more about God from another person's perspective. An elaboration of the specific cultural practices that reflect God's image in each culture is outside the scope of this book.

4. Every person and culture is affected by our sin nature collectively and individually. The influence of the sin nature drives the CbJS of our cultural type and distorts the image of God individually and collectively.

5. Christian mission organizations, churches, schools and groups need to identify how their CbJSs replace biblical truth so that they can foster biblical multicultural teams where individuals from different cultures thrive and flourish.

6. Although this book can be read for personal enrichment, it is most effective when used in conjunction with open discussions with colleagues or friends from other cultures in a community or workplace environment.

This book developed out of my own journey of discovering how the CbJS of my cultural type replaced God's truth by distorting His image. When my husband and I returned home after 25 years of cross-cultural service, I had an opportunity to do graduate studies in culture. I had experienced much cultural stress throughout my overseas experiences, and the classes were great therapy for me. However, during the first year of studies I was diagnosed with breast cancer. When I first heard that I had cancer I was very upset and thought God was punishing me. Perhaps I hadn't work hard enough for God while I was overseas. Maybe there was something about me that God didn't like. I also wondered if God considered women inferior to men. I thought through various reasons that might explain why I experienced so much stress in my role as a woman (wife, mother, household manager).[6]

In addition to studying culture, I took some Bible and theology courses and learned that God's view of me was much different than I had believed when I grew up. I came to realize that God was not constantly watching to see if I did enough work for Him or waiting to punish me if I did something wrong. Instead God loves me for who I am because He created me in His image. God intends that my thoughts, actions, and emotions reflect Him and His characteristics and He is the one who gives me the strength and wisdom to be and act in the way He intends.

In one of my courses I discussed the house floor plan of my childhood with a woman from one of the countries where I had served. When I saw the house floor plan of her childhood home, I began to realize why I experienced so much stress in her culture. I could see how many cultural patterns were reflected in the house floor plan and how useful the house floor plan was to understand cultural differences. The process of going room by room through my childhood home helped me understood how the CbJS of my cultural type was shaped and how I unintentionally followed my cultural type instead of biblical truth.

Later I began to develop a course to address cross-cultural stress using the concept of the image of God and Mary Douglas' theory of culture, along with a family tree and a house floor plan. As I worked through the lessons myself, I came to understand how my CbJS and its false beliefs about who God was, as well as who I was, had led to so much cross-cultural stress. I had thought my personal cultural beliefs were biblical, but I couldn't understand why I could not resolve my stress. Over a period of time and through periods of reflective prayer, I could identify the false beliefs of my cultural type and how they had replaced biblical truth. This revelation was a like a breath of fresh air. I no longer had to work to gain God's love, but could rest in the fact that God loved me unconditionally for who I was—created in His image. The change for me was like a conversion experience all over again. I no longer have to fill my schedule with so many things that I could never complete. Rather I am developing the practice of asking God for His wisdom day by day. Now God is helping me to take the focus off of myself and to enter into His ministry of reconciliation with my brothers and sisters from other nations, languages, and cultures (if you are interested in one of my multicultural team building workshops contact me at shersilzer@aol.com). The goal of this book is to help you foster biblical multicultural teams by replacing the CbJS of your cultural type with biblical truth. May God receive the glory.

Chapter 1

WHAT IT MEANS TO BE CREATED IN THE IMAGE OF GOD

A PERSONAL REFLECTION ON GOD'S IMAGE

When I lived overseas I would get upset with the people who worked in my home. It seems I would have to constantly tell them how I wanted things done. If I didn't watch them every minute, they would do things the way they did before. I would also get upset when they would ask me for money for school fees for their family members and money for medicine. I thought they were just spending their money on non-essential things rather than saving it for their major expenses. Although they were all adults and some were even older than me, I felt like their mother having to keep telling them how to do things. Although I knew it was not biblical to be upset with them, I felt my opinion was right because they did not seem to know how to properly budget their money. I suspected they shared their money with their friends and family so they could ask me for more. Now I realize that it was my CbJS that was validating my beliefs about money and my opinion that a person should work to cover their expenses rather than share with others. Because I also considered my beliefs biblical, I felt my negative thoughts, words and actions towards them were justified.

T his chapter is the most important chapter of the book because it discusses what it means to be created in God's image. Being made in God's image means we are each a beloved person for who we are not for what we do. Being created in God's image means that there is something about us that God considers good (Genesis 1:31). This goodness is reflected in our everyday actions that are based on what Christ has done for us. When we rely on God's will that is based on God's truth and guided by the Holy Spirit, the fruit of the Spirit abounds in our lives, and the body of Christ functions harmoniously.

If we do not believe or cannot accept that we are unconditionally loved by God because we are made in the image of God, it will be difficult for us to accept or to relate well to people from other cultures. We will have difficulty accepting cultural differences if we do not believe that we and others are created in the image of God. Unfortunately, our culture (and other cultures) promotes many different false beliefs about who we are. We have each been socialized to unconsciously think and believe that we are worthwhile only if we live up to our respective cultural standards rather than because God loves us unconditionally because He created us in His image.

When we are in the midst of cross-cultural misunderstandings or conflicts in a multicultural workplace, we don't often think about who God intended us to be. We can only think of the wrongs that other people have committed against us, and, if we are honest, the negative feelings or behavior we have demonstrated to others. Although we recognize that these are not the feelings or behavior God intended, we somehow feel justified because we believe our way is biblical and, therefore, other ways must be wrong.

In order to understand our response to cultural differences, we first need to understand who we are as God intended us to be as created in His image. Once we can accept yourself as God intended, it is easier for us to accept others. When we understand how much we are in need of Christ's redemptive work on the cross, we can embrace others as similarly in need of God's love. This understanding will also open our mind to how our cultural practices can prevent us from reflecting God's image. All human cultures have both positive and negative elements, reflecting God's image in some ways and fostering false beliefs in other ways.

Although there initially was only one language, multiple languages came into existence after the Fall when people tried to be like God and built a tower to make a name for themselves (Genesis 11) (Smith and Carvill 2000, 7-8). From the beginning, God's desire was to unite people from every language and culture through the person and work of Christ. This complete unity will take place in Heaven around the throne when people from every nation, language, and tribe will praise and worship God together (Revelation 5:7; 7:9). However, God also desires people to experience this unity now (Ephesians 4:3).

In order to move towards the unity that God desires, we each need to understand who God is, what it means to be made in the image of God, how the image of God works, and how sin can distort the image of God.

WHO IS GOD?

We will not be able to fully understand who God is this side of Heaven. However, Scripture gives countless descriptions of who God is and how God acts. He is the Creator of the world and everything in it (Genesis 1). God not only created the world, but also keeps the world and the people in it alive (Colossians 1:16-17; Acts 17:28). Our very existence is only possible through God the Creator, who sustains the life that was first breathed into Adam (Genesis 2:7).

As Creator, God is all-powerful, and nothing is impossible for Him (Luke 1:37). God's wisdom and knowledge are much greater than human wisdom and knowledge (Romans 11:33), and God's foolishness is wiser than human wisdom (1 Corinthians 1:25). What we consider righteous is just filthy rags (Isaiah 64:6).

God is also holy (Psalm 99:9), righteous (Daniel 9:7), and just (2 Thessalonians 1:6). He is light and life (John 1:4), and there is no evil in Him (Psalm 92:15). God is like no one else. He not only created us, He also loves us so much that He sent His Son to die for our sins and provide a means of salvation for us (John 3:16) so that we can be conformed to Christ's image (Romans 8:29).

God is also described as our Father who takes responsibility for us as His children (Isaiah 64:8; 2 Corinthians 6:18). As a human father makes decisions for the care of his children, so God takes care of us. He takes responsibility for us and desires to be our authority figure and decision-maker. God can also be understood by knowing Christ—the Word, the Truth, and the Way (John 1:1; 14:6). Christ set the example for us through His obedience. He became a human being so that He could die for our sins (Philippians 2:5-11). Christ lived the truth in His earthly life and as such sets an example for us to do the same. God the Holy Spirit guides us and teaches us the things we need to say and do (Luke 12:12; John 14:26; 1 Corinthians 2:13). He can guide our behavior and enable us to demonstrate the fruit of the Spirit— love, joy, peace, patience, kindness, goodness, faithfulness, gentleness, and self-control (Galatians 5:22-23)—in our interpersonal relationships.

What It Means to Be Created in the Image of God

There are three main views of what it means to be made in the image of God—the substantive, the functional, and the relational (Saucy 1993, 22-23). These three views (See Figure 2) reveal the characteristics of God: 1) as authority (2 Corinthians 6:18), responsible for decision making (e.g., giving the Law); 2) as responsible for creation (Colossians 1:16) and truth (John 14:6); and 3) as responsible for community (1 Corinthians 12:13). When we reflect the image of God in these three ways, God, rather than us, receives the glory.

The substantive view of the image of God sees the image of God as a basic characteristic of human nature, in particular our human will (i.e., the ability to make choices or decisions). The functional view of the image of God relates to how humans fulfill God's command to take responsibility for creation. The relational view of the image of God focuses on how humans reflect God through relationships with God, with our fellow humans, and with God's creation. These three views are explained in the next sections.

Substantive View - Choosing to Depend on God

The substantive view of the image of God sees the image of God as something very basic to people, that is, something that uniquely distinguishes people from the rest of Creation—the freedom of choice or the will. Humans are different from the rest of creation (Hoekema 1994, 68-73).[7] God created us with the ability to be like Him by being able to choose between good and evil (Genesis 3:5). Just as Adam and Eve had the opportunity to choose to follow God's commands or to disobey them, we also have the ability to choose to obey or disobey God's commands. Through our will we choose whether to depend on God or to rely on our own wisdom or knowledge (Proverbs 3:5-6).

James (1:5) emphasizes that we need to depend on God because we lack godly wisdom and knowledge. Therefore, God gave laws to follow that lead to righteousness (Exodus 22; Matthew 5-7). God commands us to submit to His will (James 4:7) and to follow His will instead of relying on our own planning (James 4:15). God has given His Word as a standard to follow for life and health (Exodus 34:32; Ecclesiastes 12:13; Matthew 19:17) and He has given His only Son to provide salvation that cannot be achieved by human effort (John 1:12; John 3:16).

God's standard is based on His character of holiness. The Bible repeatedly states that these laws are based on God's holiness and that God is the one who makes us holy (Leviticus 11:44-45; 1 Peter 1:16). God "who has saved us and called us to a holy life—not because of anything we have done, but because of his own purpose and grace." (2 Timothy 1:9).

The substantive view of humanity made in God's image can be seen in our choice to depend on God's wisdom instead of human wisdom (i.e., your Culture-based Judging System). When God's wisdom is used instead of our wisdom, God is glorified.

Functional View—Taking Responsibility for Creation

The functional view of being made in the image of God is when we take responsibility for creation (Genesis 1:28; Colossians 1:16-17). Some theologians refer to this aspect as dominion—the responsibility God gave Adam and Eve to rule over and care for the earth and the creatures on the earth (e.g., the fish of the sea, the birds of the air, plants) (Genesis 1:26-30). God entrusted to us the care of creation as His representatives (Hoekema 1994, 67).

After Adam and Eve disobeyed God's command, they suffered the consequences of their disobedience. Eve was to experience pain in childbearing. Adam was to rule over her (Genesis 3:16), but he would have increased labor in working the soil (Genesis 3:17). Their disobedience not only affected human relationships with God, it also affected the creation which is now in bondage to decay (Romans 8:19-20). In order to reverse the effects of sin caused by Adam and Eve's disobedience, God gave His Son the responsibility to reconcile all things back to Himself by making peace through His blood shed on the cross (Colossians 1:20). For this role Christ as the Word became flesh (John 1:14). He is also the Way, the Truth, and the Life (John 14:7). His role not only included the reconciliation of God's relationship with humanity, but also the relationship with creation—the world, plants, and animals. God's Son set the example for humanity through His life on the earth—His care for creation and His care for humanity. He also gave to believers His ministry of reconciliation (2 Corinthians 5:18). In order to take care of creation in the way God intended, we need to base our thinking on God's Word and His truths.

The functional view of the image of God relates to God the Son's role in taking responsibility and care for creation and can be evaluated on the basis of whether or not what we do and say is in line with God's truth (1 Corinthians 3:13). When we take responsibility and care for Creation in the way God intended, God is glorified.

Relational View—Loving One Another in Community

Hoekema (1994, 75-82) describes the relational view of the image of God in terms of human relationships with God, others, and creation. Human relationships are described as forming the Body of Christ (1 Corinthians 12:13) in which the particular roles and functions of believers are like parts of a body that function in unity according to the gifts God has given (1 Corinthians 12:7). Each person has a gift that enables the whole body to function properly (1 Corinthians 12:12). Therefore, everyone should have equal concern for one another (1 Corinthians 12:25) and should honor or treat members that are weaker or considered less honorable with special care (1 Corinthians 12:22-24). One member cannot say that they do not belong (1 Corinthians 12:15), and another member cannot say that they do not need other members of the body (1 Corinthians 12:21).

Human social relationships that reflect the image of God demonstrate a respect for human life (Genesis 9:6) and preserve life through words and actions (James 3:9). These relationships are also characterized by God-like love (Matthew 22:39; Luke 10:27; John 13:35, 15:12; 1 Corinthians 13; 1 Peter 1:22; 1 John 4:7). This love does not take into account social distinctions such as ethnicity, status, or gender, as all have been made one in Christ (1 Corinthians 12:13; Galatians 3:28); instead, these relationships reflect unity and oneness in Christ (John 17:11; 1 Corinthians 12; Ephesians 4:13). The fruit of the Spirit (love, joy, peace, patience, kindness, goodness, faithfulness, gentleness and self-control)are also evident in these relationships (Galatians 5:22-23).

The image of God is reflected through both genders (Genesis 1:26-27). One gender by itself is not sufficient to reflect God, but needs the other to fully reflect God. The two gender roles are not to be competitive or to elevate or subjugate the other. Rather, there is to be a mutual submissive relationship to each other based on reverence for Christ (Ephesians 5:21).

God created us so that His love could flow into us and through us to others (1 John 4:11-12). Love and reverence for God are characterized by certain kinds of responsibilities that foster healthy and godly relationships. Husbands are to love and respect their wives and be the head of the wife *as Christ is head of the church* (Ephesians 5:23-25; 1 Peter 3:7). Wives are to submit to their husbands *as to the Lord* (Ephesians 5:22; 1 Peter 3:1-6). In the same manner, children should obey their parents *for this is right* (Ephesians 6:1-3). Fathers are not to exasperate their children, but to bring them up in the training and instruction of the Lord (Ephesians 6:4). Slaves are to obey their masters with respect, fear, and sincerity of heart, just *as they would obey Christ* (Ephesians 6:5-8). Masters are to treat their slaves *in the same way, since God is the master who doesn't have favorites* (Ephesians 6:9). Obedience is not on the basis of having to be submissive, but on wanting to please God.

We are commanded to be loving, compassionate, humble, living in harmony with each other, and repaying with blessing rather than evil for evil or insult for insult (1 Peter 3:8-9). The believer is to put religion into practice by caring for family members—parents, widows and orphans (James 1:27). In this way parents and grandparents are repaid. The family member who does not provide for his or her family is said to have denied the faith (1 Timothy 5:8). Older men and women are to be responsible for the younger men and women (Titus 2).

The relational view of humanity created in the image of God enables us to fulfill the roles God has assigned and God's character is reflected in these relationships. God the Holy Spirit guides us into truth (John 16:13). The manner in which these roles are fulfilled can be evaluated by the evidence of the fruit of the Spirit, by the proper functioning of the Body of Christ, and by God being glorified.

How the Image of God Works

Just as God has various characteristics, so we also have distinct capacities that God intended to reflect Him. The English Scriptures use several words to describe these capacities. We are to love God with our whole being—heart, soul, strength (Deuteronomy 6:5); heart, soul, and mind (Matthew 22:37); heart, soul, mind, and strength (Mark 12:33, Luke 10:27) (Arndt and Gingrich 1957,404).[8] The integration of the concepts of will, mind, and heart in Hebrew and Greek reveal that the "heart" is center of the self and "the place where faith takes root in both mind and emotion" (Elliott 2006, 131). However, in English the words will, mind, and heart do not overlap in the same way. As a result, English speakers have more difficulty integrating decision making (will), thinking (mind), and emotions (heart).

The human capacity to make decisions reflects God as the ultimate authority. In English, this capacity has been called the will. As people live together, they create certain kinds of decision-making processes. 1) Some groups are characterized by individual decision making. 2) Other groups establish a system of rules that is diligently, while 3) others follow a hierarchical structure in which the ultimate authority resides at the top and those underneath submit to the will of the leader(s). 4) In other cultures decisions are made by group consensus in which every member is given a voice and has the right to speak. In the event of a disagreement, individuals defer to others in order to maintain a sense of harmony.

When our will is aligned with God's will based on God's Word, we will choose God's will over human systems of rules, human decisions made by authority figures, and human group consensus (Acts 4:19, Peter before the Sanhedrin). If we desire to reflect God's image, we will seek God's wisdom in making our everyday decisions. In this way, our will/decision making can reflect the image of God.

The human capacity to know truth (the mind) and take responsibility for this truth can also reflect God. God's truth encompasses who He is and what He has done for all of Creation. However, human knowledge is very limited. Knowledge is also culturally defined. 1) Some cultures separate knowledge and behavior. In these cultures, each person makes his or her own decisions about what is true, while 2) in other cultures knowledge is based primarily on scientific facts that can be proven through established procedures. Any deviation from scientific facts is not considered true knowledge or truth. 3) Cultures that correlate knowledge with behavior also view knowledge as that which is passed down from parent to child from generation to generation. 4) Others define truth as not only what is said, but also what is done.

When we are aligned with God's will, we make decisions based on the truth of God's Word that reflect God's character in your actions and relationships. We demonstrate a life of holiness that is not limited by cultural interpretation; a life that transcends culture.

The human capacity for relationships (the heart) reflects God's character by creating a unified community. Such a community includes rather than excludes. Human cultures tend to establish certain roles that include some people but exclude others. Some cultures elevate some people over others. For example, in some cultures strangers and outsiders are not welcomed. In others, men fill leadership roles, while women are expected to submit to their authority; the first-born son is expected to take care of his mother when his father dies while others are not; younger siblings are expected to submit to their older siblings.

When our multicultural social interactions and work team interactions align with God's truth, our decision making helps us function as part of the body of Christ utilizing our God given spiritual gifts. We accept and develop our spiritual gift/s and foster the recognition and appreciation of the gifts of others, facilitating unity and the harmonious functioning of the body of Christ. We will attend to those who are weaker and encourage them to be strong. We will attend to the needs of orphans, widows, and the oppressed (Isaiah 1:17; Luke 4:18). We will encourage the strong to lift up the weak. The fruit of the Spirit will be demonstrated in our behavior. The result will be that God is glorified (Romans 15:6, 1 Peter 2:12).

Being created in the image of God means that we can reflect God in three ways: 1) substantially, by choosing to follow God in decision making and not depending on human wisdom; 2) functionally, through appropriate care of creation based on God's truth, giving God the glory rather than humans; and 3) relationally, through the development of a loving community. The result of the image of God functioning as God intended will be a community where God's character of justice, righteousness, faithfulness, and love make a *shalom* community possible (Swartley 2006, 22-30). This *shalom* community practices repentance, forgiveness, and reconciliation (Turner 1989, 1); exhibits the fruit of the Spirit; functions as the Body of Christ; and addresses conflicts biblically.

Shalom, the Hebrew word for peace, refers not only to external peace (i.e., the opposite of war), but also to an internal state (White 1973, 4). The wellbeing or wholeness of an individual can only be fully realized within the wholeness of the community. Righteousness and justice ensures the general health and wellbeing of the community as a whole (Waltner 1984, 145).

> "The way things ought to be" in its Christian understanding includes the constitution and internal relations of a very large number of entities—the Holy Trinity, the physical world in all its fullness, the human race...In a shalomic state each entity would have its own integrity or structured wholeness, and each would also possess many edifying relations to other entities (Plantinga 1994, 10).

The image of God works to create a *shalom* community where the physical, emotional, and spiritual wellbeing of all are addressed. It would be a place where family relations and multicultural teams work together harmoniously, recognizing the strengths and values in each person and appropriately addressing differences. A *shalom* community...

> would include, for instance, strong marriages and secure children. Nations and races in this brave new world would treasure differences in other nations and races as attractive, important, complementary. In the process of making decisions, men would defer to women and women to men until a crisis arose. Then with good humor all around, the person more naturally competent in the area of the crisis would resolve it to the satisfaction and pleasure of both (Plantinga 1994, 11).

Unfortunately, this is not the way things are. Instead, there are constant misunderstandings, emotional upheavals, and unresolved conflicts distorting the image of God. That is not the way God intended things to be.

How the Image of God is Distorted

God created us to reflect Him, but we also have the capacity to develop our own ways of doing things—the varieties of human cultures. God created us, so He knows all about us. God knows what kind of relationships foster and develop His characteristics. God gave the Ten Commandments, the "Golden Rule," and other instructions in Scripture to bring life (Luke 10:27-28). Not following God's commands leads to sickness (Exodus 15:26). Being made in God's image means we have the ability to create our own culture, our own way of doing things. These human systems do not always lead to life, health, and prosperity and therefore distort the image of God. Whatever does not lead to *shalom* is sin. It "is the disruption or disturbance of what God has designed" and, therefore, does not give glory to God (Plantinga 2004, 16-17).

We unconsciously distort God's image by following our cultural practices. This occurs when we follow human systems of decision making rather than God's decision making, when we uphold human truth rather than God's truth, and when we do not function as the body of Christ or demonstrate the fruit of the Spirit. We often follow cultural ways that distort, rather than reflect, God's image.

Romans 1:18-32 explains the process involved when the image of God is distorted. First, a decision is made to not glorify God or give Him thanks (Romans 1:21). Then God's truth is exchanged for a lie (Romans 1:25). Finally, all kinds of sinful behavior result (Romans 1:29-32). The nature of sin is rebellion against God and His revelation of Himself. God allows us to experience the natural consequences of our sin (Johnson 1992, 125). However, the image of God can be restored by giving glory to God, replacing lies with the truth, and joining with Christ's ministry of reconciliation (2 Corinthians 5:18) that involves repentance and forgiveness from God (1 John 1:9) and with mankind (Matthew 6:12). This process creates and maintains a *shalom* community.

Knowing and believing we are made in the image of God and that He loves us unconditionally because of what He has done for us, not for what we do for Him, is the first step toward dealing with cultural differences. When we accept what God has done for us, we are able to accept others as God has accepted us. We are also able to understand how what we say and do can distort God's image in us and in our relationships with others. As a result of believing we are made in God's image, we desire to reconcile ourselves with God and others by repenting of our wrongful treatment of others and forgiving others when they treat us wrongly.

AN EXAMPLE OF A DISTORTED IMAGE OF GOD

A turning point in my life was when I began to understand what it means to be created in God's image. That is, that God loves me unconditionally, not based on what I do or do not do, but based on what He did for me on the cross. I came to understand how my false beliefs drove me to do more work than I was physically, emotionally, and spiritually capable of doing. As a result of my decisions I experienced a lot of stress, frustration, hurt, upset feelings, and anger.

As I meditated on what it means to be created in the image of God, I began to realize that I had distorted the image of God with the false belief that God was only pleased with me when I did a lot of things for Him. Not only did I believe a lie about myself, I also realized how proud I was of all the things I did. My pride increased when I compared myself to others. I even tried to make others work harder by suggesting ways they could add more work to their already busy schedules. I now know I offended many people with my suggestions that they do more, but my busyness validated my belief that this was the way to please God. My pride also affected my decision making as I was driven to do more and more things. Because of my drive to do so much, I didn't know how to say "no" or to discern if particular opportunities were what God wanted me to do. I thought God wanted me to say "yes" to every opportunity. I also felt justified in being angry with others who didn't accept my suggestions of things to do. Furthermore, when I had too many commitments, I couldn't fulfill them well, and that made me feel bad about myself. I couldn't see the negative circular reasoning of my false beliefs and I would project my negative feelings on others and make them feel bad as well. I didn't realize that I was distorting God's image in my decision making, my thinking, and my relationships with God and people. I definitely was not experiencing God's *shalom* nor was I fostering a *shalom* community. I didn't know that it was my cultural type with its faulty CbJS that created a negative downward spiral in my life similar to the pattern described in Romans 1.

In the next chapter I explain how the CbJS of each cultural type works to reinforce cultural beliefs about who we are.

Exercise

...1A: The Image of God

1. In light of the 3 views of the image of God, discuss how you can reflect God in these 3 ways.

2. What aspects of your life seem to contradict being created in the image of God?

3. In your opinion, are there some cultural practices that do not reflect being created in the image of God? Give examples and explain why.

Reflection #1:

Image of God

1. In light of being created in the image of God (Genesis 1:26-27) and the multicultural throng in Heaven (Revelation 5:9 and 7:9) critique what Ephesians 4:17-24 say to you about how the image of God can be reflected now in your decision-making (will), thinking (truth), and your heart (sensitivity to others).

2. How do your responses to cultural differences of co-workers need to change to reflect God more clearly?

3. Share with someone what God is telling you and pray for one another.

Exercise

...1B: Further Questions for Reflection and Discussion

1. What is the significance of all people being made in the image of God? Are there some cultures that exhibit "more" of the image of God? Less? What aspects of your own culture do not reflect God's ideals?

2. How did you become a Christian? If your parents or other ancestors were believers, how did Christianity come into your family? How do your present day family members view Christianity? How do various family members react to your personal faith?

3. What is your definition of sin? In what ways does your concept of sin reflect your cultural values? Which aspects of your own culture/family do you consider sinful?

Chapter 2
HOW THE CBJS WORKS

To understand how the CbJS of your cultural type replaces biblical truth you first need to understand your cultural type and how it works. Your cultural type develops over a period of time when you repeatedly do things in the same way. These repeated actions become comfortable and unconsciously become your preferred way of doing things.

To maintain this preference, you follow your automatic and unconscious CbJS. That is, when you encounter different cultural ways of doing things, you decide (judge) that your preferred pattern is right and that other patterns are wrong. You do this by making seemingly harmless statements or observations that point out how others do things differently, such as "They eat with their fingers" or "She has an interesting outfit." You imply "I would never eat with my fingers" or "I would never wear that outfit." You also judge people by not spending time with them or doing things together because their differences make you feel uncomfortable. You make excuses such as "I can't understand their English" or "How can anyone eat that kind of food?" You can also displace your emotions of being upset, frustrated, or even angry with people who are different. You justify these negative actions and feelings because you believe your way of doing things is the right way. Your expectation is that others should do things "your way," which, of course, is the "right way." This is our CbJS at work.

The fact that you have a CbJS is part of being created in God's image. You have the ability to decide what is right and what is wrong, just as you can choose to accept or reject others. If your CbJS aligns with God's Word and God's truth, your interpersonal relationships will reflect the harmonious functioning of the body of Christ that demonstrates the fruit of the Spirit—love, joy, peace, patience, kindness, goodness, faithfulness, gentleness and self-control (Galatians 5:22-23). If your CbJS does not align with God's Word and God's truth, your interpersonal relationships will be characterized by all sorts of evil—"sexual immorality, impurity and debauchery; idolatry and witchcraft; hatred, discord, jealousy, fits of rage, selfish ambition, dissensions, factions and envy; drunkenness, orgies, and the like" (Galatians 5:19-21). The following is an example of my cultural bias or CbJS at work.

A Personal Example of the CBJS

When I lived overseas I would get upset with the people who worked in my home. It seems I would have to constantly tell them how I wanted things done. If I didn't watch them every minute, they would do things the way they did before. I would also get upset when they would ask me for money for school fees for their family members and money for medicine. I thought they were just spending their money on non-essential things rather than saving it for their major expenses. Although they were all adults and some were even older than me, I felt like their mother having to keep telling them how to do things. Although I knew it was not biblical to be upset with them, I felt my opinion was right because they did not seem to know how to properly budget their money. I suspected they shared their money with their friends and family so they could ask me for more. Now I realize that it was my CbJS that was validating my beliefs about money and my opinion that a person should work to cover their expenses rather than share with others. Because I also considered my beliefs biblical, I felt my negative thoughts, words and actions towards them were justified.

To help you better understand how your CbJS works, you will study a description of the Structure and Community theory of culture that describes how different cultural types function. I will also explain how the four cultural types have a cultural bias that is maintained by its CbJS and how the CbJS distorts the image of God.

What is your Cultural Type?

Mary Douglas, a well-known British social anthropologist, developed a model of culture after studying a number of cultures around the world, from isolated tribal communities (in Africa and Papua New Guinea) to modern industrial cultures (e.g., in Britain). She views culture as a way of organizing information that people use to view the world (Douglas 1992, 33). She discovered that cultures tend to define themselves along two dimensions—how people are different from one another (Grid) and how they are similar (Group). (Douglas 1982, 183-254).[9] In this material I use the terms "Structure" and "Community" adopted from R. Daniel Shaw.[10] Structure (Grid) refers to the characteristics that differentiate individuals in a group; Community (Group) refers to the similarities that define people as belonging to a community. The combination of these two dimensions form four basic types of culture (Thompson, Ellis and Wildavsky 1990, 8, Lingenfelter 1997, 25):[11]

Individuating	**Weak Structure and Weak Community**
Institutionalizing	**Strong Structure and Weak Community**
Hierarching	**Strong Structure and Strong Community**
Interrelating	**Weak Structure and Strong Community**

Each of these four cultural types places a different emphasis on the dimensions of structure and community characterized by different decision-making styles, different beliefs, and different kinds of social responsibility for others. These four cultural types present a helpful framework for understanding how the Culture-based Judging System (CbJS) of each type distorts the image of God.

Douglas states that these four types can describe all cultures. We will follow her general concept, but we also recognize that cultures can change, and that people can be influenced by more than one type (e.g., with the influence of globalization, consumerism, immigration, etc.). The focus here is for you to understand which of the four types most accurately describes your own culture to help you foster a biblical multicultural team or community. This book will guide you through a series of exercises to help you discover how the CbJS of your preferred cultural type works and compare it with biblical truth.

Douglas' model provides a useful framework for understanding cultural types. Differences or distinctions between individuals are referred to as Structure. Differences can be made on the basis of status, age, gender, birth order, ethnicity, color, job position, or other categories. The type of decision making (individual, system, consensus) reflects Structure. The type of social responsibility (individual responsibility, system responsibility, or group responsibility) reflects Community.

Douglas says that individuals unconsciously adopt Structure and Community ideals through habit patterns formed by their everyday activities. Although these unconscious cultural ideals are not generally verbalized or discussed, they can be observed in a person's daily behavior patterns and how they respond to different ways of doing things.

Structure focuses on differences or distinctions; Community focuses on similarities. Structure sets up social roles that differentiate individuals. As such, Structure focuses on the external, material, and physical aspects of the people. Community, in reinforcing the similarities among individuals, focuses on the internal, immaterial, and spiritual aspects of people. Structure is established by decision making type—following the authority system (the rules of the system or group consensus or tradition) or making individual decisions. Community is established by participation within a community—upholding the community identity, giving in to community pressure, taking social responsibility for group members, etc. Structure, in differentiating individuals, forms a system of legal justice; Community, in reinforcing similarities of the community, forms a system of social justice. Figure 1 summarizes the main features of Structure and Community.

STRUCTURE	COMMUNITY
Sets up social roles that differentiate individuals	Establishes similarities through community participation
Focuses on the external, material, and physical aspects of individuals	Focuses on the internal, immaterial, and spiritual aspects of the community
Makes decisions based on individual or system rules	Makes decisions based on community consensus
Forms a system of legal justice	Forms a system of social justice

Figure 1: Main Features of Structure and Community

Structure and Community tend to be either strong or weak in a given culture; that is, a culture has either a high degree or a low degree of structure or community. In Strong Structure cultures people follow the rules of the system and the authority of the leaders, but in Weak Structure cultures people tend to make their own rules. Strong Community places social pressure on individuals to conform to the community norm, but in Weak Community groups the individual does not need to yield to social pressure or conform to community norms.

Structure

Structure not only categorizes people, it also forms authority systems through different kinds of decision making processes.

Structure differentiates people through social roles such as status, gender, age, birth order, color, ethnicity, and job position. Some cultures differentiate people on the basis of inherited social position, such as those with royal blood or higher status positions. Some Asian cultures, for example, follow a Confucian hierarchical order of ruler>subject, husband>wife, parent>child, older>younger, friend>friend to maintain social stability that views the family as reflecting the order in the universe (Tu 1998, 123). Thus, within a Confucian society there is ideally respect and submission by the subject to the ruler, wife to husband, children to parents, younger to older, and friend to friend. In this system the role of the firstborn son is to carry on the family name and to take responsibility for the family's wellbeing. Many Latin American cultures have a hierarchical social structure based on color (white-European, mixed white, brown-Native American, and black-African ancestry (Stephenson 2003, 27). Many African cultures have a social structure based on ethnicity, status, color and gender.

In the United States workplace individuals are differentiated by job title and/or the status of their job position. Presidents and/or chief executive officers have the highest status positions and consequently receive the highest salaries and have the largest offices. There are various levels of administrators below them, each with responsibility in different areas. The workers underneath the administrators are also differentiated by job title and salary. Cultures with a number of socially held distinctions are defined as Strong Structure; cultures with fewer socially held distinctions are defined as Weak Structure. Within the business, government, and educational systems, the United States functions as Strong Structure even though corporations/institutions are not the same. However, these work distinctions are not always carried over into United States social situations as they are in Strong Community cultures.

Structure is also formed by how decisions are made, where authority lies, and who wins in conflict situations. Structure has two kinds of decision-making processes—following the rules of the system (Strong) or individual decision making (Weak). Structure also has two types of authority—invested in the authority figure (Strong), in which the system always wins in conflict; or invested in the individual (Weak), where the individual with more power wins (See Figure 2). Each type of decision making forms the basis for habit patterns that influence how a person fulfills everyday responsibilities as well as how they interact socially.

	Strong Structure	**Weak Structure**
Type of Decision Making	Following the rules of the system	Decisions based on individual choice
Type of Authority	Invested in the authority figure	Invested in the individual
Result of Conflict	System is always right	Individual with more power/influence wins

Figure 2: Main Features of Structure and Community

Decision making in Strong Structure follows the rules of the system. In this system there is an established way of doing things or rules that have developed over time. These rules have been formalized into policies and are difficult to change. The system gives power to the authority figures to interpret the rules of the system, and people are expected to follow the rules. Therefore, the typical result of disagreement in Strong Structure cultures is that the system always wins. On the other hand, Weak Structure cultures emphasize individual decision making processes. In Weak Structure individuals find their own sources of information upon which to base their decisions, whereas in Strong Structure cultures the information already exists in the rules of the system or as interpreted by its leaders. When individual decisions are made in Weak Structure cultures, the individual holds the authority, but when Weak Structure individuals disagree, they do not have the support of Strong Structure to resolve the disagreement. When the individual has the authority, the rules are interpreted individually. In Weak Structure cultures individuals have their own opinions and, as a result, there is constant disagreement and conflict. The typical result of conflict in Weak Structure is that the person with more power or influence wins.

Community

Community refers to the strength of social relationships demonstrated by social cohesiveness and responsibility for community members. Strong Community is based on the belief that individuals are basically spiritual beings connected to a higher power in the universe. Life functions appropriately when there is harmony among the community members, including their relationship to the created world and even to deceased family members. The spiritual connection is demonstrated through on-going reciprocal relations between individuals including sharing resources—physical, emotional, spiritual. The image of family relationships (e.g., children to parents) is often used in other areas of life, including the work situation. That is, employees may refer to their superior as their father or mother, and employers may refer to their subordinates as sons or daughters.

In Strong Community cultures life is viewed as a cycle of significant life events. Lifecycle events (birth, puberty, marriage, death), as well as the agricultural calendar (new year, new moon, planting, harvesting, etc.), are celebrated as a community to insure the continuance of harmonious and prosperous life. Regularly helping one another and reciprocating help fosters the cycle of life. Not helping or reciprocating causes bad things to happen. Strong Community individuals, therefore, need to participate regularly in social activities to maintain the harmony of community life. Good and evil, right and wrong are defined by community participation. Participating and helping others is good and right; not participating and helping others is evil or wrong. Individuals who do not participate in social activities are viewed as inviting or causing misfortune. Individuals who do not participate with the community may also be suspected of manipulating the spirit world through black magic, sorcery, spells, etc. that cause bad things to happen. Therefore, the community takes responsibility for group participation in community activities in order to promote good and avoid evil.

Families are very important in Strong Community cultures because a person's identity is derived from belonging to a family and/or community. Loyalty is first and foremost to one's family; other affiliations take second place. Individuals in Strong Community spend time together regularly and by so doing demonstrate their loyalty. Resources are shared, and individuals who extend help also expect reciprocal help from others at some time in the future. This reciprocity continues beyond the present generation, thus strengthening family or community ties and relationships.

Strong Community decisions are supported by consensus among community members. Such consensus reinforces community cohesiveness. Community decisions also foster accountability. People who do not participate equally are encouraged by the other group members to participate. The individual does not generally make his or her own decisions, but follows the decision of the community because they identify with the community.

On the other hand, Weak Community individuals define people in terms of individual characteristics (skills, wealth, possessions, etc.), rather than belonging to a community (nationality, ethnicity, family, group, etc.). Individual skills, physical characteristics, and material possessions take precedence over other factors. Instead of one strong community affiliation, Weak Community individuals may have multiple affiliations, but no overriding loyalty to one community. There is also no standard for family relationships. Some individuals have frequent interactions with their family members; others have little or no affiliation with family members. Weak Community individuals tend to engage in activities either individually or with a variety of communities—more typically with non-family members than family members. As a whole there are no common characteristics of Weak Community.

Individuals exhibit Weak Community when they have the choice of deciding which social functions to attend. They may decide not to attend a good friend's birthday party because they want to do something else. Reciprocity is not normally expected in Weak Community, as sharing of resources is an individual preference and not a social obligation. People in a Weak Community culture use a verbal or written "thank you" to respond to a gift or kind deed to signify the end of the transaction. No further reciprocity is needed (Stewart and Bennett 1991, 94). Good and evil are also defined individually, with no standard definition of what constitutes good and evil or right and wrong. What is right for one person might be considered wrong for another. The important thing is everyone has the right to establish his or her own system of right and wrong. Weak Community individuals can make individual decisions or can follow a system of rules. Weak Community individuals take little or no social responsibility for others. They believe social responsibility is an individual matter.

In Strong Community the individual is defined in terms of spiritual characteristics such as belonging to a family or a community; in Weak Community the individual is defined in terms of physical and external characteristics such as roles, skills, achievements, or material possessions (See Figure 3). In Strong Community group rights take precedence over individual rights; in Weak Community individual rights take precedence over community rights. Strong Community fosters social responsibility, whereas Weak Community fosters individual responsibility. In Strong Community the community takes responsibility for its members; in Weak Community the individual does not generally take responsibility for others.

Strong Community	Weak Community
Individual defined by belonging to the community	Individual defined by physical, external characteristics as roles, skills, achievements, possessions
On-going reciprocity	Kind deed ends with "thank you"
Community participation is right (good) and not participating is wrong (evil)	Individual standard of good and evil, right and wrong
Community rights take precedence	Individual rights take precedence
Community takes responsibility for its members	Individuals take responsibility for themselves

Figure 3: Strong Versus Weak Community

Weak and Strong Structure and Weak and Strong Community form four different types of cultures: Individuating, Institutionalizing, Hierarching, and Interrelating. The characteristics of each of the four types are described in the next section.

Four Types of Cultures

The two types of STRUCTURE (Strong and Weak) and two types of COMMUNITY (Strong and Weak) form four types of cultures (See Figure 4 and 5):

Individuating (Weak Structure and Weak Community) is characterized by cultural activities based on individual choice

Institutionalizing (Strong Structure and Weak Community) is characterized by cultural practices based on following the rules of the system and of authority figures

Hierarching (Strong Structure and Strong Community) is characterized by cultural practices based on loyalty to a hierarchical system

Interrelating (Weak Structure and Strong Community) is characterized by cultural practices based on community principles of equality.

Individuating Culture

Individuating cultural practices reflect little social differentiation (Weak Structure) and little social similarity (Weak Community). The ideal individual in this type of environment is an autonomous, independent individual whose identity is based on his or her own accomplishments, possessions, skills, and characteristics. The Individuating ideal is based on a person's right to choose his or her own identity rather than being given an identity from being part of a system or group. Individuating people also prefer to choose their level of social responsibility (Naylor 1998, 51).[12] Innovation and creativity are highly valued in this type.

When Individuating people are classified as a group, it goes against their individuating ideal. Therefore most US Americans[13] will deny that they have a culture or that they share the same cultural ideals with other Americans (Naylor 1998, 19,22). The Individuating system is typically found in industrial cultures that have their economic basis in free enterprise (e.g., US, Netherlands, etc.) (Hersman 1995, 174). This ideal is reflected in sayings such as "looking out for #1" and "I did it my way." The focus of Individuating is cultural practices that center on the individual and not on the community or the rules of a system. The general US American culture is an example of an Individuating culture. Individuating values independence.

However, an Individuating culture is difficult to maintain if everyone does what they want to do without regard for others. This would be chaos. Therefore, institutions help Individuating regulate choices and provide some societal order. The US American has to conform to institutions such as the local government, but they can choose to move to another area and they can also choose to affiliate with other institutions (e.g., church, social club, sports group, etc.) (Douglas 1992, 58).

Institutionalizing Culture

Institutionalizing cultural practices are characterized by a system of social differentiations (Strong Structure) with little social similarity (Weak Community). The ideal individual in this type of environment is an individual whose identity comes from following the rules of the system and obeying authority figures rather than an identity in relationships with others or making one's own decisions. By fulfilling a particular role, a person maintains an identity associated with a role that keeps interaction with others to a minimum. The purpose of the structure is to create an environment in which more work can be accomplished. This type can be described as having a "cubicle" mentality, as most Institutionalizing offices assign individuals in lower positions to windowless cubicle work cells, while those in higher positions have larger offices with windows. The cubicle walls minimize social distractions. Institutionalizing cultures focus on profit via work rather than on relationships with others.

The Institutionalizing type of social environment is found in many parts of the world, particularly among large communities of people that require a rigid structure to maintain order. This type ranges from the pluralist Western world that facilitates the isolation of individuals and even of ethnic communities from one another (e.g., US [Douglas 1992, 28], Britain, Germany) Douglas 1992, 28, Lingenfelter 1998) to dictatorial regimes that subjugate its people to its will.[14] This type suppresses creativity and innovation by forcing its people to conform to the particular rules and regulations of its system. A large country may have Institutionalizing national practices, but be made up of smaller ethnic groups with stronger community features.

In an Institutionalizing culture a typical individual exchanges personal freedom for identity in the system. This person is afraid of making individual decisions, preferring to follow the rules of the system. Individuals in this type may develop fatalistic tendencies from having to continually submit to rules and be fearful of challenging the system or authority figures. These individuals not only hold to the rules of the system, they also consider themselves failures when they do not follow the rules. Although these individuals have three options—challenge the system, suppress negative emotions about the system, or submit—the last two are the most common responses. Individuals know that it is very difficult to change the system, therefore, they become submissive and develop fatalistic attitudes (e.g., as seen in authoritarian religions, Western institutional systems, and Confucian social systems). Institutionalizing values submission.

Hierarching Culture

Hierarching cultural practices are characterized by strong social differences (Strong Structure) and strong similarity (Strong Community). This type differs from Institutionalizing in that the individuals are part of an organized whole that functions in coordination with each part. Although Hierarching is similar to Institutionalizing, Hierarching individuals find their identity through belonging to the community rather than through following a system of rules. This identity is reinforced by regular participation in unifying activities that reinforce community identity (unlike the lonely person in Individuating and Institutionalizing cultures). Hierarching prioritizes the interaction of the community over work and profit. It discourages innovation and creativity in order to maintain the status quo. This type has a centralized structure of individual units that form levels that form an organized whole. Each unit has its head, and the members in each unit ideally support the decision of the head. The head does not make decisions that he or she knows are not supported by consensus of the unit. If the community disagrees with the head, they make a community effort to express their disapproval, often going around the authority of the head to that person's superior.

Each unit in a Hierarching group is connected to the next higher level through its head. The person in this type is neither autonomous nor independent, but finds identity from being an integral part of the whole structure. Each person in this type knows his or her place in relationship to the others and derives security in functioning appropriately in his or her place. Decision making follows the order of the hierarchy and each unit affected by a decision is, ideally, consulted in the decision making process. This type can accommodate large numbers of individuals within a stratified structure. Thus inequality is part of the definition of the whole. This type fosters harmony and respect for persons and is found more frequently in kin-based economic cultures (e.g., cooperatives of ethnic communities such as in Indonesia or single ethnic communities such as the Japanese, Koreans, some Chinese communities, and the O.T. Israelites) (Wildavsky 1984).[15] This type values a hierarchical community.

Interrelating Culture

Interrelating cultural practices are characterized by a combination of little social differentiation (Weak Structure) and strong similarity (Strong Community). This type differs from Hierarching in that there is no stratified structure. Instead, each individual is considered equal to the others. This type can have traditional complementary roles such as male/female, right/left, sacred/secular, etc. This type seeks to maintain equality through dialogue and sharing. This community reacts against organizational rules, regulations, and authority figures (as is the case in Australia[16]) (Mosler 2002, 94). The important concept in this community is equality or complementation, and this principle becomes the basis for decision making. Sharing of physical possessions or equal exchanges are important in this type. The community ostracizes people who deviate from the norm.

Leaders are not highly valued in this type unless they maintain a semblance of order by their charismatic personality. Leaders typically discount their leadership role and identify themselves with the other members of the community. The on-going dialogue regarding equality is necessary to maintain community identity. Interrelating communities are typically small, because maintaining equality over large number of individuals is difficult. Interrelating communities often arise as a response to the inequalities of the organized structures (Institutionalizing & Hierarching) around them, and the lack of community similarities and competition in Individuating. This type fosters equality of resources (e.g., Australia) (Hersman 1995, 153), although Interrelating cultures are more typically small special interest communities (Atkins 1991) or small groups where sharing resources is important. This type values equality.

The four cultural types provide a framework for understanding cultures through two main dimensions—Structure and Community. These two dimensions form four basic cultural types, but do not necessarily describe everyone or everything in a particular culture. Nevertheless, you are encouraged to discover which type best describes you so that you can understand how your CbJS or cultural bias works in distorting the image of God.

Cultural Type	Structure/Community	Characteristics
Individuating	Weak Structure, Weak Community	Identity based on comparison of self with others' skills, possessions, and achievements Individual decision-making, does not focus on social interaction Fosters creativity and innovation Values independence and autonomy
Institutionalizing	Strong Structure, Weak Community	Identity from following the rules and submitting to authority Focus on an individual's role rather than on interaction with others Fosters submission to rules Values submission
Hierarching	Strong Structure, Strong Community	Identity from belonging to an orderly structured whole Fosters interaction with others, but discourages creativity and innovation Fosters harmony and respect of persons Values a hierarchical community
Interrelating	Weak Structure, Strong Community	Identity based on an on-going dialogue of who is in and who is out Fosters interaction with others, but leaders are not highly valued Fosters equality of resources Values equality

Figure 4: Characteristics of the Four Types

Structure and Community Theory

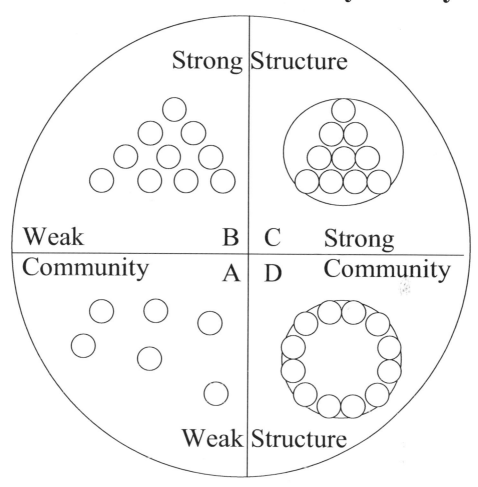

Figure 5: Four Types of Cultural Ideals

HOW THE CBJS OF YOUR CULTURAL TYPE WORKS

Mary Douglas refers to the preference for doing things one way over other ways as cultural preference or "cultural bias" (Douglas 1982, 183-254). The strength of our bias depends on the extent to which our identity is associated with our preference. Cultural bias is maintained by our CbJS. You can see this at work when you encounter cultural differences when your normal way of handling things does not work. Your CbJS is your will, mind, and heart at work; it is how the image of God functions in you. When you encounter cultural differences, you automatically have an emotional response. If you respond positively to the difference, you can exhibit the fruit of the Spirit (love, joy, peace, patience, goodness, etc.). If you respond negatively to the difference, you may be surprised, upset, shocked, or even angry. Your emotional response is generally accompanied by an action that reinforces your emotion—inclusion or exclusion, acceptance or rejection, joy or anger, etc.

If you dislike an experience because it is different from your own set of beliefs, you will validate or justify your beliefs with your words, actions, and feelings. This is also your CbJS at work. The strength of your CbJS depends on the degree to which your cultural type is part of your identity. The greater your identity is aligned to your particular cultural type, the greater your emotional response will be to cultural differences. As a result, you begin to justify your negative responses to these differences through various explanations and actions.

Your family (and societal) expectations of right and wrong shape your CbJS. The words and actions that uphold your cultural ideal are rewarded; the speech and actions that do not uphold your cultural ideal are discouraged, not rewarded, and sometimes even punished (Douglas 1982, 190). In this way, your family and culture unconsciously shape and maintain your cultural bias.

Douglas says the best way to understand your cultural preference or bias is to examine your responses when things go wrong or do not go as you expect. Each cultural type has different explanations for why things go wrong and has different ways to that correct what goes wrong (Douglas 1992, 5). Your explanations and actions are your CbJS at work. These explanations and actions validate your cultural type. The Individuating type seeks to validate the uniqueness of the individual; Institutionalizing culture validates the rules of the system in order to have order and produce work; Hierarching validates the hierarchy of the community while fostering solidarity; and Interrelating validates bonding insiders together against outsiders through principles of equality (Douglas 1992, 137). Just as you are rewarded for upholding your cultural ideal, you can unconsciously use your CbJS to punish others for not upholding your cultural ideal. Your CbJS justifies negative responses (stress, frustration, complaints, anger, etc.) towards those who do not follow your cultural type.

Your CbJS makes repeated judgments (with words or actions) of what is right and what is wrong in order to validate your way of doing things. It is a natural and human response to deal with differences. Although your words may not sound like a judgment, what you say highlights a difference—a different way of speaking, interacting, eating, working, etc. Your actions also indicate a judgment—avoidance, delaying interaction, or even retaliation. The reason for pointing out the difference is to validate your way of doing things.

The Individuating CbJS upholds the belief that self-focus is the ideal through repeated acts of individual decision making and repeated individual choices concerning social responsibility. In order to maintain their individual identity, individuals point out how they are different from others and talk about their own achievements, successes, or failures (Naylor 1998, 61-62).

Douglas says that the typical sins of the Individuating person are greed and pride in the self with little or no responsibility of others (Douglas 1992, 145). Therefore, Individuating people reinforce their ideal by talking about themselves in order to enhance their individual identity. They also believe that acquiring the latest technology, clothing, car, etc. enhances their individuality. Individuals also take advantage of opportunities to get ahead. However, the Individuating person's desire for control can easily lead a person to take advantage of others, to hurt them, or to cause others to lose out. These behaviors help the individual to get ahead. They are not considered wrong because the Individuating person's self-focus has little or no awareness of how their actions affect others (Wilkins and Sanford, 2009, 42).

The Individuating CbJS validates individual choice and individual responsibility. Individuating people tend to be surprised, shocked, or angry when people do what they are told to do and do not challenge the rules of the system (Institutionalizing), when people do not make individual decisions but follow the traditional hierarchy along with group pressure (Hierarching), or when people want to share resources equally or in a complementary manner (Interrelating).

Individuating people feel justified when they get upset with top-down decisions, social hierarchies, or principles of equality because they believe it is morally wrong to not have individual choice. To deal with an injustice, Individuating people blame others, the situation, etc. when things go wrong. This cultural justifying process reinforces the Individuating cultural ideal summarized in the saying "Rules are meant to be broken."

The Institutionalizing CbJS upholds the Institutionalizing ideal by following a set of rules with individual choice for social responsibility. That is, they prefer to choose which social responsibilities to have rather than be told what to do. When the focus is on following a set of rules, habit patterns focus on the individual's ability to fulfill the rules. The rules become more important than the people affected by the rules. It is very difficult for Institutionalizing individuals to understand the downside of the rules because their focus is on following the rules. They assume that rules are right, and, therefore, the consequences of the rules are just. Institutionalizing people have learned to not question the rules. They do not take into consideration personal situations that may adversely impact an individual. In summary "Rules are rules."

Douglas says that the typical sin in Institutionalizing cultures is to not demand justice and to silently accept the consequences of the system (Douglas 1992, 145). Institutionalizing cultures focus on upholding a system and don't question the rules of the system. When things go wrong for the Institutionalizing person, the system cannot be blamed because the Institutionalizing person's identity is based on the existence of the system. If an individual disagrees with the rules, he or she is challenging his or her own identity. Therefore, when an ideal is not achieved Institutionalizing people assume that the established norms or rules upheld by the structure or leaders were not followed. The Institutionalizing person then develops a strong desire to uphold the system and at the same time develops a fatalistic attitude that "nothing can be done" to change the system. The Institutionalizing slogan is "You can't fight city hall."

The Institutionalizing CbJS validates following the rules of the system and submitting to authority figures. Institutionalizing people tend to be surprised, shocked, or angry when people do not do what they are told and challenge or try to get around the rules of the system (Individuating), when people use community pressure to follow the hierarchical order (Hierarching), or when people do not follow the rules of the system and challenge the authority figures about inequality or the lack of complementation (Interrelating).

Institutionalizing people feel justified in getting upset with individual decisions, social hierarchies, and principles of equality because they believe it is morally wrong to not follow the rules of the system and submit to authority figures. To deal with this injustice, Institutionalizing people blame others for not following the rules or submitting to authority figures when things go wrong and are blind to the injustices of their system. This cultural justifying process reinforces the Institutionalizing cultural ideal.

The Hierarching CbJS validates respect for the distinctions within the hierarchical status differentiation and loyalty where community members take responsibility for each other. Because the strength of the community develops a sense of belonging, social relationships take precedence over rules. This ideal fosters working together and utilizing top-down strengths for the good of the community. Community members take responsibility for the lives and work of its members. However, this type can also take advantage of interpersonal relationships when higher status individuals demand service from lower status individuals as reciprocation for granting special privileges. Individuals who do not follow the will of the community are also punished more severely, because their actions disrupt the harmony of the whole. The focus on the community also results in less achievement and fulfillment of goals than in the Individuating and Institutionalizing types. Douglas says that this type, in focusing on the good of the community, can often lead to a kind of inappropriate community pride, which tempts its leaders to enhance their position through getting more of the resources (Douglas 1992, 145). The typical sin in Hierarching is unhealthy community pride.

When illness, accidents, death, losses, or natural disasters occur, they are perceived as disruptions to the natural order and harmony of life. These misfortunes are believed to arise from a lack of harmony within the community or a lack of loyalty by one or more community members. When a person performs an action that benefits him or herself rather than the community, he or she is perceived to invite something bad to happen to the community as a whole. Lack of loyalty and disrespect to community members also invites mishaps. Such actions need to be punished in order to restore the community's harmony. The community takes responsibility to address these wrong situations appropriately by identifying and punishing the individual who deviates from the community norm. The Hierarching community motto is: "This is how it has always been done."

The Hierarching CbJS validates the unity of the group as a whole following the established hierarchy. Hierarching people tend to be surprised, shocked, or angry when people do not follow tradition or do not show respect to authorities (Individuating), when people do not rely on community support (Institutionalizing), or when people reject the orderly rules of the system and challenge authority figures about the inequality of the system (Interrelating).

Hierarching people feel justified in getting upset with people who make individual decisions, follow the rules of the system, or adhere to principles of equality. To deal with an injustice Hierarching people blame the ones who take initiative and don't follow the social hierarchy when things go wrong. They are also blind to injustices of their system. This cultural justifying process reinforces the Hierarching cultural ideal.

The Interrelating CbJS validates following principles of equality with community responsibilities and upholds equality in all aspects of life. The strength of this type is support of the community members to see that each person gives and receives equally. People in Interrelating (and Hierarching) cultures are never lonely, because they always function within a community context. The Interrelating community, however, does not rely on traditional boundaries to define those who are in or not in the community. Instead, they rely on an on-going dialogue that continually defines and redefines community membership on the basis of an individual's actions. Individuals who do not follow the will of the community are ostracized and generally not readmitted into the community. Leaders do not lead from a position of ascribed authority, but by their charismatic personalities. An accepted leader is one who continually emphasizes that he or she is just one of the community.

Douglas says that the typical sin of Interrelating is envy. People in Interrelating cultures easily recognize inequalities and constantly try to equalize situations and resources so that their ideal of equality can be maintained (Douglas 1992, 145). The Interrelating ideal is violated when resources are not equally shared or reciprocated. Because equality is the ideal in this type, any form of inequality, particularly as demonstrated by a hierarchical (Institutionalizing or Hierarching) type, is seen as opposing the group ideal and needing correction. Harmony arises from equality, and equality is demonstrated through the sharing of resources.

The Interrelating CbJS validates equality within the group. Interrelating people tend to be surprised, shocked, or angry when people do not share or when they take more than others (Individuating), when people insist on following the rules of the system or blindly following authority figures (Institutionalizing), or when people support the inequalities of the hierarchical system (Hierarching).

Interrelating cultures feel justified in getting upset with individual decisions, following the rules of the system, and following the social hierarchy. When things go wrong Interrelating cultures blame the people who take initiative, people who follow the rules of the system, or the social hierarchy. They are also blind to the strengths of the other types. This cultural justifying process reinforces the Interrelating cultural ideal. This type is exemplified in the "tall poppy syndrome" where those who stand out are knocked down.

In each of the four cultural types there are different patterns of decision making and social responsibility based on the beliefs that create a cultural bias or preference against the other types. When a cultural type is not upheld, it justifies negative emotional responses and actions. Each CbJS seeks to maintain its ideal.

These four cultural types form either a legal or a social system of justice (See Figure 6) that establishes right and wrong. Therefore, people in each type treat those who do not live up to the same ideals in a negative way. These negative reactions are not considered wrong; they are considered just. However, as human systems of justice, they deviate from God's standard of justice and idealize behaviors that do not exhibit the fruit of the Spirit or the appropriate functioning of the body of Christ. Each cultural type has a built-in system that distorts the image of God.

As each of these types have a preference for a particular type of decision making (individual, system, consensus), they tend to follow the particular kind of decision making of their cultural type. This is based on human truth rather than God's truth. The result is that some people are treated better or worse than others, resources are not shared equally, and individual focus replaces focus or concern on the group as a whole. The CbJS of each type reinforces human beliefs and each of these types can distort the image of God in three ways:

Decision Making (individual, system, tradition, or principles of equality)

Truth (individual, system rules, tradition and hierarchy, and principles of equality)

Heart (individual responsibility or social responsibility)

Examine yourself to see whether your response to cultural differences demonstrates your CbJS or a dependence on God based onGod's truth and a love for others that strengthens the community.

Structure-Legal Justice	Community-Social Justice
Institutionalizing The individual is blamed for not following the rules of the system or the authority figures that represent the system.	**Hierarching** The community identifies and punishes the individual who deviates from the hierarchical community norms and invites misfortune to the community.
Individuating The individual blames everyone and everything else when he or she does not live up to their Individuating ideal.	**Interrelating** The community continues to dialogue about equality in order to redistribute resources equally.

Figure 6: Systems of Justice

How a CBJS Distorts the Image of God

As an American I can be characterized as an Individuating person. When I was overseas, I felt the social pressure that people put on me to attend various social functions. I preferred making my own decisions about whether to attend a particular event. I didn't like people making decisions for me (e.g., what functions I was going to attend or what food I was to eat). I liked to be in control. I did not like the group pressure or being made to feel responsible for others.

As an American I was also treated as a higher status person. I was given a better seat, better food, and more attention. I believed people should be treated equally and that I should not receive any preferential treatment. There were also things people expected of me in return, but I never did quite figure out how to behave as a higher status person in their culture. Not knowing what was wrong and not knowing how to address these issues was very stressful for me. It made me unsettled and unhappy. My unhappiness showed in my face as well as in my relationships. I complained a lot to my American co-workers about how strange this non-American culture was. I knew my actions were not biblical, but I thought my cultural values were biblical and that justified my negative behavior. However, I couldn't understand why I didn't feel better about myself if I was "right."

After learning about cultural types, I realized that my way of doing things was an Individuating cultural way rather than a biblical way. I had responded to cultural differences according to my Individuating culture, justifying my Individuating value by pointing out all the people and situations that prevented me from fulfilling my Individuating ideal of being successful (by doing things the way I wanted, when I wanted). I complained about the local culture that valued Strong Structure differentiation. I complained about the Strong Community social pressure to conform. I complained about my organization and about co-workers who didn't do their part to help me succeed. When my stress was the greatest I did not want to interact with others because I felt they all contributed to my stress. I was playing out my CbJS according to my cultural type. My decision making was to judge the others as wrong because I had already judged my individual decision-making belief as right and justified getting upset and even angry with the people whom I had come to serve. I had distorted God's image in my will, mind, and heart.

Exercise

...2A: *Model of Culture*

1. What are some categories you use to differentiate people (e.g., age, education, gender, physical characteristics, personality traits)? In what ways do these differences effect how you relate to other people?

2. Are you more comfortable with Strong or Weak Structure? Why? Give an example.

3. Are you more comfortable with Strong or Weak Community? Why? Give an example.

4. Are you more comfortable with Strong or Weak Community? Why? Give an example.

❧

Culture Based Judging System Question #1:

Cultural Type

Choose the response that best describes you. I prefer...[17]

___ 1. making my own decisions based on the information I find and choosing who to be responsible for.

___ 2. following the rules of the system and choosing who to be responsible for.

___ 3. following tradition and having the group take responsibility for its members.

___ 4. following group consensus and having the group take responsibility for its members.

❧

Reflection #2:

Theory of Culture

1. Think about one of the cross-cultural misunderstandings with your co-workers that came to mind while going through this session/module.

2. Identify the beliefs of the cultural types in regard to this misunderstanding.

3. Read the following verses and explore how your responses to your co-workers' cultural differences can be more biblical:

   Genesis 11:1-9; Judges 12:6; Luke 14:7-11; Acts 6:1-4; 1 Corinthians 12:13; Galatians 3:28; Colossians 3:11

Chapter 3
HOW THE CHILDHOOD FAMILY SHAPES YOUR CBJS

UNDERSTANDING MY CHILDHOOD UPBRINGING

I was the second of four children and the only girl. My older brother was only 18 months older, but my two younger brothers were seven and eleven years younger. I was not taught to take responsibility for my older brother, and we competed for our parent's attention and approval. We would also tell our parents when the other one disobeyed or didn't do their work well. On the other hand, I was expected to look after my two younger brothers as an adolescent.

My parents had a set of rules that we had to follow. If we broke the rules, we were punished with a spanking as that was acceptable then. My parents did not give us much praise because they thought praise would make us proud, but they did compare us with one another hoping to improve our behavior by comparison. I felt my older brother was treated better than I was, and I didn't think that was right. This often led to bitterness towards each other and towards our parents.

Because I was the only girl, I was the only one who was expected to help my mother with housework. That is probably the reason I grew up disliking housework. I would complain about my parents to my age mates because I had to take more responsibility being the only girl.[18]

After considering my childhood upbringing, I began to see how different factors influenced the person I am today and why I respond in the way I do to authority figures and to my co-workers.

Our childhood home influences our adult life in many ways. If you came from a large family, you may feel more comfortable interacting with a variety of people. If you were an only child or one of two children who didn't have to play or work together, you may have more difficulty interacting with others. If sons were preferred over daughters, you may automatically take that cultural practice with you into present day situations and accept male preference in the workplace. However, if males were not treated differently than females in your childhood family, you may be disturbed when you see men getting preferential treatment in the workplace. Similarly, the way you were rewarded and punished by your parents helped to form your CbJS. You typically learn to behave in ways that were rewarded and generally avoid punishment if possible.

Revisiting your childhood family can help you understand how you developed a preference for doing things in certain ways. If what you learned in your childhood home is reinforced by society, it tends to become the "correct" way of doing things. When your way of doing things is challenged, you feel justified in feeling angry. Your upbringing shapes your present day response to conflict—your way is right and the other way is wrong (Naylor 1998, 23-24). Revisiting your childhood family can shed light on your present-day misunderstandings and conflicts, as well as provide insights on how to address present day relationships biblically.

In order to show how your childhood family contributes to your CbJS, this chapter explains family structure and nurture/discipline in relation to Structure and Community. I will also show how my own family's CbJS distorted the image of God.

The Family

Each culture defines family in its own way. A family is normally defined as blood related people who live together in the same home, generally parents and their children. However, some families may include extended family members, as well as others who live in the home (e.g., household employees in Mexico) (Standish and Bell 2004, 66). Some cultures limit a family by the age of the children. When an American child turns 16, 17, or 18 (depending on the State), they are considered an adult and can be on their own to establish their own family (Althen 1988, 51). In many African, Asian, and Latin Strong Community cultures a child remains a child until his or her parents die, even if the children are married and have their own children.

Strong Community culture families stay together for longer periods of time tend to spend more time together on a regular basis and take more social responsibility for each other. They also help each other with household chores rather than assigning individual chores as in Weak Community cultures such as the United States.

Exploring the roles and responsibilities of family members sheds light on the different definitions of the family. Family roles are differentiated in a number of ways, physically as well as socially. Higher-status family members may be given special seating, spoken to with special words, or shown respect by nonverbal signals such as lowering one's head or bowing. Age, gender, social position, and generation may define social status (parents have higher status than children, grandparents have higher status than parents, etc.).[19]

One way to discover some of these differences is to look at the terms of address used within the family and the responsibilities associated with them. Another way is to compare responsibilities based on birth order and gender in the childhood home. Examining Structure and Community aspects of the family will also help you understand how families function.

Terms of Address

In Weak Community cultures a person is addressed by a first name (as in the US), but in other Strong Community cultures people are identified by their family name (e.g., in Japan: Takagi-san, belonging to the Takagi family). In Korean churches a pastor is identified by a term that identifies his order in the hierarchy from senior pastor, associate pastor, to youth pastor. In other cultures people are addressed using the name of their firstborn male child, e.g., "Michael's mother" or "Michael's father" or according to their birth order, e.g., firstborn, second born, etc. The appropriate term of address is determined by cultural ideals.

Kinship relations define roles culturally. In the United States the terms "mother" and "father" are normally used to refer only to a person's biological mother and father. Along with these terms are certain assumptions of the mother's or father's role. The Yanomamo of Brazil and Venezuela use "father" and "mother" to refer to a father's brothers and a mother's sisters or to a father's sisters and a mother's brothers.[20] In the United States parent's siblings are referred to as "aunt" and "uncle." Mothers and fathers have the primary responsibility for the care and nurture of children; aunts and uncles do not. Cultures with multiple "mothers" and "fathers" also have more people to take responsibility for the care and nurture of the children. People in some cultures refer to non-related older people in the same community who are older as "aunt" and "uncle."

In the United States people call their blood siblings "sister" or "brother." Other cultures extend the use of these terms to refer to the children of parents' siblings ("cousins" in the United States). Some cultures differentiate only between male and female siblings (e.g., brother and sister), while others differentiate between father's brothers' children[21] (parallel cousins) and father's sisters' children (cross-cousins) and mother's brothers' children (cross-cousins) from mother's sisters' children (parallel cousins). Other cultures have different terms for older and younger sisters and brothers (e.g., Indonesia and Japan). Different kinship terms may also indicate those one can and cannot marry (e.g., cross versus parallel cousins). Some cultures use the term "sister" and "brother" for those who are not blood related, but share other things in common such as religious beliefs.

In Hawaii a person's mother and his or her father's sisters are referred to as "mother" and the person's father and father's brothers are referred to as "father." Their children all call each other "brother" or "sister," making one big family depending on the number of one's parents' siblings. Status is also determined by genealogical seniority rather than by generation, age, or sex (Hand and Pukui 1998, 43). Thus a person could be older than someone he/she calls "father."

Weak Structure cultures, such as the United States, do not tend to have stable or long-term family structures. Parents may divorce and remarry and combine and re-combine family members into new family units. In this case a child would have one or more sets of parents (step-mothers or step-fathers) along with their birth mother or birth father. In addition to their biological siblings, they would also have step-sisters and step-brothers, as well as half-sisters and half-brothers.

In some cultures the siblings of one's parents may call their siblings' children "daughter" or "son," while others may call them "niece" or nephew." In Korea, Turkey, and some African countries, there is a different term for each relationship.[22]

In some parts of Asia, family terms are extended to non-family members who interact with family members on a regular basis. The terms "mother" and "father" and "children" may also be used in the workplace. Supervisors refer to those under them as their "son" or "daughter" and workers refer to their supervisor as "mother" or "father." Along with the extended use of family terms come expectations for reciprocal responsibility for each other similar to the actual family. Some cultures have a role for godparents, who may not have a blood relation to a child, but are given certain responsibilities for a child.

Each CbJS will uphold the proper use of the terms of address. Not using the appropriate kinship term results in some form of correction and/or punishment.

Birth Order

Family functioning can be influenced unconsciously by how parents treat their children according to their birth order. As such, birth order can have a great influence on what the child will be like (Leman 2004).

Firstborn children are often expected to take more of a leadership role with their siblings. As a result, firstborn children generally tend to be more focused, responsible, and finish activities more quickly. Other children who have received special treatment for one reason or another may also be more like a firstborn. Middle children with a larger age span between them and their older siblings can also have firstborn characteristics. Normally, middle children join an already established family system and tend to receive less attention. As a result they tend to be more compliant and take less initiative, because they have an older sibling who has already been given responsibilities. Middle children often feel less important than the firstborn. Lastborn children tend to get less attention because their parents have gotten older and older siblings have been put in charge of them. Parents might not be as strict with their younger children as they were with the older children. Lastborn children may also develop special skills to get attention to compete with their older siblings. Parents may also have a special emotional bond with their last child knowing that there won't be others.[23] In some cultures the lastborn child is expected to take care of the parents when they get old.

Asian cultures highly value the role of the firstborn son. He is expected to take the leadership role in the family after the father dies and to care for his widowed mother. He is also the one who passes on the family name. Therefore, Asian parents put more effort into ensuring the success of the firstborn so he can successfully fulfill his role of caretaker of the family name. This role can be so burdensome that girls may avoid developing a relationship with a firstborn son, because they realize that the majority of the firstborn son's responsibility tends to fall on his wife. The oldest son also takes care of the family inheritance, sometimes sharing it with his siblings.

Birth order is emphasized in some naming systems. In Bali, children are given a name specifying their birth order from first to fourth (the fifth child is given the term for firstborn and so on). In Scandinavian countries the oldest son or daughter may be given the name of their parent or grandparents to reinforce the family connection.

The importance of birth order in a culture is reflected in the rituals and celebrations held around the birth of the first born child, particularly a son. Other cultural customs such as the redeeming ceremonies for Jewish sons[24] may also reinforce the value of the firstborn.

If children do not follow the cultural ideals for birth order properly, their parent's CbJS will correct and/or punish them.

Gender

Each culture has its own ideal for girls and for boys. The role of a girl and a boy in a culture will be shaped by the expectations of what their role will be as an adult. Traditionally, the girl's role is to imitate her mother, who takes care of her children and home, while a boy's role is to imitate his father, who takes care of his family by working outside the home. These expectations create different social expectations for males and females. The social expectation for men might be on the physical ability to work outside the home, while the social expectation for women might be on the social ability to be a homemaker and to care for children inside the home. However, globalization has created more options for jobs for both males and females and has changed parental expectations for their children or changed children's expectations of what jobs they can have.

Gender roles may also be traditionally associated with cultural and religious concepts of cleanliness. In some cultures menstruation of women places them in a category of unclean or impure. According to Mernissi (1987, 40), women may be regarded as impure, of a lower status, having more of an animal nature, being socially subservient in public, and having an orientation towards children. Since a basic function of women is reproduction, they are viewed as having more of an animal nature. In Muslim and Hindu cultures, the roles for females and males are associated with concepts of cleanliness and purity. Males are considered clean, while females are considered dirty. The male role is to be a protector of the females. Public space is male space, while domestic space is female space. Males are also associated with equality, reciprocity, connection, unity, communion, brotherhood, love and trust, while females are associated with inequality, lack of reciprocity, segregation, separation, division, subordination, authority, and mistrust.

When space allocated by gender is violated, rituals may be required to restore the purity of the violated space, whether male space or female space. In Central Asia, girls ritually violate male space when they arrive at puberty, but return to female space when they are married (Shakhanova 1992, 167). In Latin America, the male fulfills his *macho* role of sexual expertise outside the home, while the female fulfills her *marianismo* role of sexual purity (like the Virgin Mary) inside the home (Brusco 1995, 79).

The strict regulations for Muslim gendered space apply only to individuals who are related, not to individuals who are unrelated.

> Muslim sexuality is territorial: its regulatory mechanisms consist primarily in a strict al-location of space to each sex and an elaborate ritual for resolving the contradictions arising from the inevitable intersections of spaces. Apart from the ritualized trespasses of women into public spaces (which are, by definition, male spaces), there are no accepted patterns for interactions between unrelated men and women. Such interactions violate the spatial rules that are the pillar of the Muslim sexual order. Only that which is licit is formally regulated. Since the interaction of unrelated men and women is illicit, there are no rules governing it (Mernissi 1987, 137).

Muslim social customs reinforce the separation of women from men. Men are not to look at women, and women are to lower their gaze in the presence of men. Women are not to reveal their adornments except to family members. In Muslim society, this custom is seen as a source of pride rather than of oppression. The ultimate form of separation is the harem, which is even more prestigious. The concept of honor and shame also regulates gender roles in Muslim cultures. In Egypt, because a man is a public figure, his honor is dependent on his wife's behavior in public, but because a woman is not a public figure, she does not depend on her husband's behavior for her honor or respect (Wikan 1984, 635-652).

In the Chinese family the concepts of *yin* and *yang* divide the world according to gender. *Yin* (female) represents the concepts of dark, softness, and the direction down; *yang* (male) represents light, hardness, and the direction up (Adler 2002, 60). Although male/female differences in the Chinese family may reflect superiority versus subordination, the Central Asian home in Chapter 5 reflects complementation. The yurt home is divided equally between the male on the left side and the female on the right side. Males place their items (hunting and musical instruments) on their side; females place their items (blankets, pots, pans, plates, etc.) on their side. The home is also divided between the secular area in front, where guests sit; and the sacred area in back, where rites of passage take place (Shakanova 1992, 167).

In other homes the kitchen is referred to as female space, but the visiting area or verandah is male space. The female area is typically close to the activities that are associated with women—cooking and certain types of production, such as basket-weaving, mat plaiting, etc. (Tjahjono 1989, 218). The public space of men may be the living room, special men's houses, public institutions (such as cafes), or open spaces. Women are oriented towards private space, the home, or the back parts of the house.

Each culture has differing expectations for the roles of men and women. These expectations can also change over time. It is important to understand the various factors of a family that contribute to the definition of femaleness or maleness. Some of the factors that contribute to the definition of gender include the household's view of reproduction, the complementation of male and female roles, and the differing beliefs about the family. Gender roles also shape marriage rituals and other rites of passage.

If appropriate gender roles are not followed, the parents' CbJS will seek to correct and or punish their children according to their cultural ideal.

FAMILY TREE

A family tree is a tool to draw family relationships, which form the environment of childhood cultural practices. Family trees can also help to clarify family medical issues and characteristics that have been passed down, both good and bad. One of the things passed down in my family has been the tendency to get cancer. Both of my grandmothers passed away of cancer (one with breast cancer and one with ovarian cancer). My father and my older brother had prostate cancer and passed away when the cancer spread to other places. My mother had breast cancer twice. I've had breast cancer and uterine cancer. I've also tested positive for a cancer gene, making it very probable that my siblings, children, and grandchildren will also have cancer.

In comparison with my husband's family, my family is very quiet in family social interactions. At a gathering of my family members, the atmosphere is very calm. At my husband's family gatherings, however, there is usually a lot of noisy talking, which at first made me think they were arguing. My family was taught not to make a lot of noise or to argue.

You may discover that certain abilities (e.g., musical, mechanical, artistic) or personality characteristics have been passed down in your family. A willingness to share this with co-workers helps increase understanding of each other.

Figure 7 shows four generations of my own family starting with my parents and ending with my grandchildren (you will be drawing your family tree in Exercise 4c).

Directions for drawing a family tree:		
Triangle " △ " for male		
Circle " ○ " for female		
Equal sign "=" for married		
Vertical line "|" for children		
Horizontal line "—" for siblings		

Figure 7: A Four-Generation Family Tree

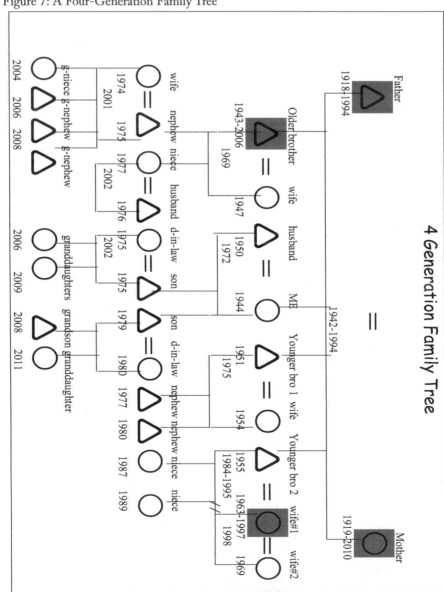

NURTURE AND DISCIPLINE

Nurture (discipline) is perhaps the area of your childhood experience that impacts youmost strongly today, as it is the major area where your CbJS was formed. When you were nurtured and disciplined during your childhood you learned how to make decisions of what was right and what was wrong. When you were taught good manners—how to speak, the kind of clothes to wear, how to go about daily activities, and how to relate to others—you learned a system of morality. The way you were taught to do things became the "right" way, and other ways were "wrong." When you are asked why you do things in a certain way, you may respond, "That is how my parents taught me" or "That is the way it has always been done" or "This is how I prefer to do things." Doing things in the same way over a period of time becomes your automatic and unconscious preference. When a situation arises and you are not able to do things in the way you normally do, you may become uncomfortable, irritated, and maybe even upset.

Children learn cultural ideals from their parents or caretakers, who use different means to reinforce their ideals. Parents train their children by telling them repeatedly how to do things or by setting an example for them to follow. When you didn't meet your parents' expectations, they would remind you in some way to correctyour behavior. If you did not follow these rules, there may have been consequences—physical, emotional, and social. Some parents remind their children using physical means such as hitting various parts of their body (top of fingers, palms of their hands, heads, backside, or legs) with an instrument (stick, belt, folded newspaper, etc.). Other parents give their children a certain disapproving look, verbally point out their mistake (scold, shame, correct, etc.), or discuss what they did wrong. Some parents might indicate their displeasure by sarcasm. Children can be isolated from others for a period of time or be scared into appropriate behavior by stories about bad or scary people harming them if they don't behave appropriately.

US American parents typically punish a child who does something wrong. Some Filipino parents punish the oldest daughter twice to teach her to be responsible for her younger siblings but only punish her siblings once. Some Asian parents punish all of the children to encourage siblings to be responsible for each other. In cultures where compliments are not the norm, parents may complimenta child (as a form of sarcasm) to let them know their behavior is not appropriate (e.g. Japan).

Parents discipline their children for various reasons. If the child understands that the parent disciplines out of love or to help the child grow up well, the child is more likely to accept the punishment as just. If the child thinks that the parent does not discipline out of love or a desire to help the child grow up well, the child will not accept the punishment as just.

The way your parents or other authority figures disciplined you in childhood influences how your present day CbJS works. The way you respond when things go wrong today most likely is the same way your parents responded when you did not live up to their standards as a child. The types of things you complain about today may be similar to the things your parents complained about when you were growing up. The way you punish others when they don't live up to your standards may be similar to how your parents treated you. Children learn the cultural ideals of their parents through the way they are nurtured and disciplined.

Because individual success is important in Individuating cultures, parents will look for areas in which a child might succeed. If one child does exceptionally well, the parents praise that child and hold him or her up as an example to the other children. When a child doesn't do well, parents can come up with a number of explanations for the child's lack of success. They can say that the child is like the other parent (i.e., it is their fault) or not capable. They may also complain about all the money they wasted on the child or compare a child negatively with another child's success.

In past generations US American parents could physically punish their children when they disobeyed. However, physical punishment is now prohibited in many areas due to the potential for child abuse. Another kind of disciplining for US American children is the use of "time out" in which the child who has not acted appropriately is removed from the location where they misbehaved. Parents use "time out" to help the child cool down and think about what happened so that he or she won't violate the rule again. The Individuating child will not normally be disciplined for upsetting social harmony, but only for his or her individual actions.

In Individuating cultures, the person who controls knowledge, reason, and/or resources is in control. This person may or may not be the father; it can be the mother or another member in the family. If a father is absent, the role may fall to the mother. If both parents have extended time away from the family, one of the children may take control. Some parents in the United States take a motivating role rather than an authoritative role. They try to entice their children to behave by offering rewards (e.g., particular foods or things a child likes) (Stewart and Bennett 1991 and Condon and Yousef 1975, 151).

Institutionalizing (Strong Structure and Weak Community) parents train their children to follow the rules. There may be clear role expectations for boys and girls and a preference given to the first-born male. These parents teach children not to question their authority. The typical answer to "why" is "because I said so." In this way children are taught to blindly follow the rules and suppress their negative emotions. Institutionalizing parenting tends to produce two kinds of children—compliant children who follow the rules but suppress their negative feelings and devious children who learn how to get around the rules. When a child doesn't do well or live up to their parents' ideal, the parents feel justified in punishing the child severely.

In Institutionalizing cultures the father or oldest male has control unless that person is absent. Then the oldest female or next oldest male tends to take control. This person will have authoritative control over the rest of the family members. The accompanying attitude is intended to be submission to the family's authority figure. The *machismo* and *marianismo* values of Latin American families exemplify the Institutionalizing worldview. For men the cultural ideal is the conquering *macho* man, whereas the cultural ideal for women is the purity of Virgin Mary by being submissive. A man can fulfill the *machismo* role by having extramarital affairs. The woman is expected to accept her husband's behavior as an innocent and pure wife even though her husband is not pure (Brusco 1995, 79). The traditional Asian woman's role is also Institutionalizing in that her role is to be submissive her whole life. She is submissive first to her father, then to her husband, and then to her oldest son when her husband dies (Tu 1998, 122).

Hierarching (Strong Structure and Strong Community) parents train their children to respect the hierarchy and the family. They are taught to let older people and higher-class people go first, eat first, and have the best food and best seats. Children are to bow and not look their elders in the eye. They are taught the importance of the group or community over the individual by learning how to be aware of others' needs and treating each other according to their status. When a child doesn't do well, he or she is shamed and punished for bringing shame to the family name. Hierarching parents may also lavish gifts on their oldest son, but have a different standard for younger siblings, whether male or female. In fact, younger siblings may be expected to take the blame for the wrong-doing of the oldest son. Physical punishment is acceptable in Hierarching cultures.

In Hierarching cultures, everyone has a distinct place in the social order and that order needs to be observed to maintain order in the universe. The father or oldest male is the natural authoritative head, but the mother's role is coordinated with the father's role in the division of labor. Gender and age are also differentiating factors in the family hierarchy. Hierarching families have strictly prescribed social roles that distinguish each person's place in society. Each person knows his or her place, and the social order continues in a harmonious fashion as each person fulfills the expectation of his or her social place and role. The ideal is belonging to a well-ordered society that takes responsibility for each other according to the traditions of the society. The child who stands out from the group is punished severely because standing out from the group disrupts social harmony and is believed to invite something bad to happen to the family and the community as a whole.

Interrelating (Weak Structure and Strong Community) parents seek to train their children to follow principles of equality. Parents train their children to share their food and resources equally and reciprocally. They teach their children to be aware of others' needs (food, clothing, rest, etc.). This applies to those who are older as well as peers and younger children. If someone doesn't share appropriately or reciprocate appropriately, retaliation or payback is culturally justified.

Interrelating parents frequently hold up negative examples of children who are not taught properly and do not follow the principles of equality. They readily point out who is and isn't sharing appropriately. If a child does something to stand out from the rest of the group, his or her parents may do or say something to minimize what the child has done.

Control or authority in Interrelating cultures is maintained through group consensus. If a child does something wrong, the group members will gossip about the child to put social pressure on the child to conform to the group's expectations.

In some Interrelating cultures in Papua, Indonesia, a family that receives a wife for their son must reciprocate by giving a daughter for their daughter-in-law's brother to marry. Wedding gifts can also be taken back if the couple does not meet the expectations of those who give the gift. When an Interrelating child gets good grades or receives a special award for academics, the other children seek to maintain equity by making fun of the student rather than congratulating him or her for individual success. Interrelating parents may also punish all their children for the wrong doing of one in order to train them to be responsible for one another.

In Mexico there are several categories of relationships that reflect Strong Community. Each of these relationships has different responsibilities. Godparents (*compadrazgo*) take responsibility in life events such as baptism and first communion. They also provide help with life situations such as moving into a new house. Best buddies (*cuatismo*), similar to twins, spend time together and share confidences. True friends (*amiguismo*) rely on each other for social needs or help in the workplace (Standish 2004, 66).

The CbJS regarding Nurture and Discipline in each of the four types upholds the cultural type. Individuating parents have different responses to their child when he or she fails to live up to their expectations. Institutionalizing parents will freely punish their children for not following the rules. Hierarching parents may punish the older child more for not taking sufficient care of younger siblings, and Interrelating parents may punish all the children equally for one child's disobedience. The explanations and actions of parents in each culture uphold their cultural type.

CBJS and the Family

The CbJS shapes how decisions are made of what is right and what is wrong. Children learn what is right and what is wrong through their nurture and discipline experience. Children are rewarded for doing the "right" things and punished for doing the "wrong" things. Through this process children learn how to make decisions based on certain beliefs. If a family's nurture and discipline align with what God considers right, the family will demonstrate godly emotional responses in their behavior and actions. However, much of a child's learning is based on cultural values that parents have learned from their parents and unconsciously pass on to their children. The nurture and discipline that reflects being created in the image of God results in godly characteristics such as love, joy, peace, etc., but the nurture and discipline that does not reflect being created in the image of God results in ungodly characteristics such as jealousy, anger, envy, etc. Revisiting your childhood family structure and how it functioned can reveal how your present day responses to cultural differences can distort the image of God through your CbJS that involves your will, mind, and heart. That is, you may get frustrated, upset, or angry at particular events and justify your emotions in one or more of the situations outlined below.

If you are from a Weak Structure family, you may get frustrated, upset, or angry when you are expected to:

- be differentiated according to birth order, age, or gender

- follow a lot of rules

- blindly submit to authority figures

- show respect to a person based on his or her position

Your belief in Weak Structure justifies:

- not making distinctions based on birth order, age, and gender

- complaining about distinctions based on birth order, age, and gender

- pointing out the shortcomings in the system

- challenging the authority of the leader

- treating people better only if they earn your respect

If you are from a Strong Structure family, you may get frustrated, upset, or angry when:

- people don't observe birth order, age, and gender distinctions

- a leader does not take an authoritarian role

- group members do not follow the rules, but try to get around or challenge the rules (or authority figure)

- older people are not greeted or addressed appropriately by title (Standish 2004, 67) or a respectful term

- others achieve higher status before you

Your belief in Strong Structure justifies:

- ignoring or punishing people who do not observe birth order, age, and gender distinctions

- replacing a leader who does not take an authoritarian role

- assigning menial tasks to or disgracing group members who do not follow the rules, but try to get around or challenge the rules (or authority figure)

- demoting a person who does not address authorities appropriately

- doing things to prevent others from achieving higher status

If you are from a Weak Community family, you may get frustrated, upset or angry when:

- people tell you what to do or try to put social pressure on you to conform

- people use your possessions without asking and don't return them unless you ask for them back

- people expect you to reciprocate a kind deed or help you received

Your belief in Weak Community justifies:

- shaming a person by confronting them publicly

- causing the group to lose face by refusing to share your resources or requiring they return what you loaned them in as good a condition as when they borrowed it

- complaining about the people who give in to social pressure and reciprocity

If you are from a Strong Community family, you may get frustrated, upset, or angry when:

- group members do not take responsibility for one another

- group members don't use social pressure to make people conform

- people don't share their resources

- people say or do things to make the group lose face

If you are from a Strong Community family, you may get frustrated, upset, or angry when:

- punishing group members who don't take responsibility for others

- gossiping about those who don't conform

- taking from others who don't share with the community

- ostracizing people who do not conform

Your CbJS can distort the image of God in your decision making, beliefs, and emotions; that is, your negative emotions, based on false truth, result in actions that hinder biblical truth being evident in your relationships.

How a Family's CBJS Distorts the Image of God

Although my parents and I were all born in the United States, we still held to many Asian cultural values. Because I did not grow up with other Asians (except my brothers), I considered myself totally American. This prevented me from understanding who I really was.

I was the second of four children and the only female child. My older brother was given special privileges because he was the firstborn male. I, as the only female child, was not given similar privileges, but was expected to care for my two younger brothers. My parents justified their actions because my brother was male and was older (by 18 months). My American Individuating side thought that this wasn't fair, but because of my Hierarching Asian values I couldn't discuss this with my parents. I was taught to obey and do what I was told. Asian women are expected to fulfill their role and to endure as exemplified by both my grandmother and my mother, who quietly submitted to their husbands. Similar to them, I had a lot of suppressed bitter feelings from being expected to quietly submit and not speak up.

My parents used a combination of Asian and American culture in disciplining us. When I didn't do as my parents directed as a young child, I was physically punished. When I was older I was sent to my room to think about what I did or had privileges taken away. However, there was not a discussion about what I did wrong or why I was punished. I knew I had disobeyed their wishes and sometimes did not think my punishment was fair, but I couldn't disagree with them because they were my parents. My older brother and I often competed for our parent's approval by telling them if the other did something wrong. When my older brother was a teenager, he began to rebel against our parents' authoritarian treatment. I felt obligated to do things to make up for his rebellion. I tried harder to make my parents feel better by getting good grades and doing more work around the house.

After I was married, my husband and I had two sons but no daughters. Being the only woman again highlighted my role as an Asian woman, to take care of the males in the family. It also reinforced my belief that God preferred males. I felt I had to work harder as a woman to please God. As a missionary I thought I had to have a full time mission job as well as take care of the household. Consequently, I was not able to do my job or my housework well. I became stressed out and depressed because I believed God was not pleased with me. I was not raised to speak about it, so I continued to suppress my negative feelings.

My husband's Anglo-American background differed from my Asian background regarding the discipline of our sons. I believed physical punishment was the right way to discipline children, but he preferred reasoning with them. As an Asian I felt it was wrong to disagree with my husband, but I also was upset because I thought my way of disciplining was the right way. Again I suppressed my negative feelings thinking that was what God wanted me to do.

Another way the Asian and American cultures were in conflict was in the way I communicated with my husband. I unconsciously assumed that my husband and I shared the same cultural values so I thought I did not need to speak directly about our misunderstandings. I thought he would know what I was thinking and I would get frustrated when he didn't. As an Asian I couldn't bring myself to speak up, so I suppressed my negative feelings once again.

When I studied the Structure and Community theory of culture and learned how the CbJS worked, I began to realize how my CbJS had justified my false beliefs and actions over the years. When I was eventually diagnosed with breast cancer, I learned that there was a connection between my Asian and American CbJS and certain types of cancer. As seen in my family tree, many of my family members had cancer. Our CbJS contributed to cancer and was passed on unconsciously. I worked harder to please God because I thought He was not as pleased with women. This, in turn, led to unrealistic expectations on my part of how much I could actually do. When I wasn't able to be successful due to these unrealistic expectations, I would feel bad about myself. The resulting stress was compounded when I suppressed my negative feelings. I repeated this cycle over and over in my life, as did my Asian family members.

When I was first diagnosed with cancer, God began to speak to me about who I was as created in His image. Studying the Structure and Community theory helped me to discover the false beliefs I had about myself that didn't reflect being created in God's image. By combining my theological and anthropological studies I began to understand how the CbJS of my Asian and American cultural types worked to maintain my false beliefs. My healing would only come through replacing my CbJS with biblical truth. Through extended periods of reflective prayer I began to see how my upbringing had distorted God's image in my decision making, my thinking, and my emotions.

In this chapter you looked at how the family is defined by different cultures. You ⌐ how Strong or Weak Structure and Strong or Weak Community define the fami₁ differently and create different expectations of the family. Structure and Community determine the roles and responsibilities for parents and children according to age, gender, and birth order. The cultural ideals are reinforced through the nurture and discipline practices that shape your CbJS. You also saw how a family tree can help you recall information about your family and about family characteristics that are passed down from one generation to another. You also saw how the CbJS of my cultural type worked to distort God's image in my life. As you think about your own background and how it shaped you, it will help you understand how others may also have been shaped in their childhood homes. This knowledge can lead to better understanding of yourself and your co-workers in the workplace.

In the next chapter you will discover how the house floor plan of your childhood home contributes to your CbJS. You will use your childhood house floor plan in Chapters 5-9 as you revisit your childhood cultural practices to assist you in discovering how your CbJS upholds your cultural type.

EXERCISE

...3A: The People in My Family

1. How many people lived in your childhood home?

2. Who were they and how were they related to you?

3. What was your birth order? (only child, first of ?, 2nd of ?, last of ?)

4. How many males were in the family? _____ females ?_____

5. Explain if any of the children received special treatment.

6. What characteristics of family life were shaped by your birth order, gender, or number of children in your family?

⤳

Culture Based Judging System Question #2:

Family Nurture/Discipline

Choose the statement that best describes the nurture/discipline in your family... [25]

_1. I was punished for what I individually did wrong. I was compared to what others were or were not doing. I was rewarded/praised for individual achievement.

_2. I was punished individually for not following the rules. I was not praised for individual achievement. It was just expected.

_3. My oldest sibling was punished more for not taking responsibility for the others. It wasn't unusual for a younger person to take the blame for an older or higher status person. We were scolded/punished if we did something to stand out or show disloyalty to the community.

_4. We were all punished equally if someone didn't share resources or cultural responsibility. We were scolded/punished if we did something to stand out or show disloyalty to the community.

⤳

Reflection #3:

Family Structure

1. Think about how your childhood family relationships with your parents and siblings formed the basis for relationships with supervisors and co-workers.

2. Read the following verses and ask God how He wants you to improve your relationships with your co-workers:

   Psalm 78:1-4; Psalm 103:17-18; Joel 1:3; 1 Timothy 5:4,8; Ephesians 6:1-4

3. Share with someone what God tells you and pray for one another.

Reflection #4:

Nurture and Discipline

1. Think about how your childhood nurture and discipline practices have shaped your present day Culture-based Judging System (CbJS).

2. Use the following verses to examine how God might want you to realign your CbJS with His Word in response to your co-workers' different ways of doing things:

   Proverbs 13:24, 23:13; Jeremiah 46:28; Hebrews 12:11; Revelations 3:19

3. Share with someone what God reveals to you. Pray for one another.

∽

Exercises

...3B: Drawing My Family Tree

Draw several generations of your family tree following the family tree directions in Figure 7 and trace family characteristics you observe. Indicate close and/ or broken relationships, Christian and non-Christians.

...3C: Learning from My Family Tree

1. What are some common characteristics in your family?

2. What good/bad traits have been passed down in your family?

3. Share your family tree with one other person.

   a.   What were some comments or questions they made about your family?

   b.   What insights did you gain about the other person?

   c.   What insights did you gain about yourself?

   d.   Pray for each other.

....3D: An Exercise of Reflection and Discussion

With a discussion partner, or on your own, reflect on these topics and how your family approached these issues during your childhood…

1. Childrearing practices. How standards are taught/enforced.

2. Courting/dating and marriage practices. Ideal mates. Ethnic/cultural preferences for marriage partners.

3. Divorce/remarriage.

4. Relationships with in-laws.

5. Life passage celebrations: birth, firsts (food, steps, haircut, ear piercing), birthdays, circumcision, puberty, anniversaries, death.

6. Comparing childhood nurture and discipline with present day leadership, management, and co-worker challenges.

Chapter 4
How the Childhood Home Shapes Your CBJS

A Personal Reflection on Home Comforts

When I lived overseas, the first thing I did was try to make my new home comfortable. I put up thick curtains that people couldn't see through instead of the local style sheer curtains. We also put screens on our windows (unlike the local houses) to keep out mosquitoes. I was also very uncomfortable with the year-round tropical heat and so we installed an air conditioner in our bedroom. I felt I needed a gas (not kerosene) stove, a refrigerator, and a washing machine to do daily chores. I knew that none of my neighbors had them, but felt like I couldn't live without them.

I never really considered how these physical comforts reinforced my role as a high status person in a Strong Structure culture. Later, when I reflected on my role as a witness for God, I began to realize that I was following Individuating ideals by making my own life comfortable first and presenting a materialistic view of Christianity rather than presenting the person of Christ. My focus on my own comfort also diminished the time and energy I had for the physical and spiritual needs of those around me.

The house you live in becomes your home. However, it isn't just the physical structure that makes it a home; it is the comfort, security, and acceptance you receive living in it. If your childhood home did not provide comfort, security, and acceptance, you may find this material difficult to process. On the other hand, it will give you an opportunity to look at areas of your life that prevent you from accepting yourself, and, in turn, accepting others.

The best way to discover your own cultural values is to live in another country for a period of time. You will quickly find there are many little things that bother you about how houses are arranged. If you take note of the complaints you have about the host culture, you will come to realize they reflect your cultural values. Individuating people complain about anything outside of their control and do everything within their control to change their living conditions. Institutionalizing people complain that things aren't made according to the proper rules. Hierarching people complain about structures that do not reflect adequate respect for elders or provide enough space for family interaction. Interrelating people complain about inequality or the lack of complementation in the layout and construction of the house.

In Chapter 1 we saw that being made in the image of God includes cultural differences (Revelation 5:7) that can be reflected in decision making that relies on God, thinking based on God's Word, and loving others in community. In Chapter 2 the four cultural types were introduced and we discussed how the CbJS of each type distorts God's image in different ways through cultural kinds of decision making, thinking, and ways of relating to others. In Chapter 3 the review of family structure and functioning (nurture and discipline) discussed how your CbJS of right and wrong was shaped and how it impacts present day relationships with authorities and co-workers. In this chapter you will discover how even your childhood house floor plan contributes to your CbJS and how it can distort the image of God.

House Floor Plans and Culture

The greatest surprise many people have living cross-culturally is that houses are shaped by culture. Amos Rapoport (1969, 46), [26] a professor of architecture, was one of the first people to discuss how culture shapes the house floor plan. Similarly, a cross-cultural study of houses found that more complex cultures were reflected in more complex house arrangements (Kent1990, 127-152). Condon and Yousef (1975, 115) discovered that not only was the "home a microcosm of culture," but a person's emotional well-being is also strongly attached to the culture learned in the childhood home. They concluded that the best way to discover culture is to return to the childhood home. Condon and Yousef were particularly concerned that US Americans were not adequately prepared emotionally to deal with the cultural differences they experienced overseas. Their article recommends people revisit their childhood home to discover the childhood cultural practices that made them comfortable (Congdon and Yousef 1975, 104).

The house floor plan is not only a tool to help you learn about your own culture, it also triggers childhood memories as you draw it, share it, and compare yourself with others. Once you learn about your own culture you will be better able to understand others.

In this chapter you will look at key elements of houses (shapes, structures, locations, house arrangement, and symbolism), at the interplay of culture and houses, and at how culture can distort God's image. Three house floor plans are presented in this chapter to illustrate Individuating and Institutionalizing, Hierarching, and Interrelating cultures. The exercises at the end of the chapter will help you analyze your childhood house floor plan, recognize your cultural type, and discover how your CbJS distorts God's image.

ASPECTS OF HOUSES

When you move to a different location, you discover the aspects of the house that make you feel "at home" or others that make you feel uncomfortable. These will be the things that you comment on positively or negatively, such as the shape of the house, the structure, the location, or symbolic features of the house.

House Shape

The two basic house shapes are round and rectangular. The round house is less common, but used by a number of people around the world—Dine/Navajo (Native Americans in the United States), Mongolians, Central Asian nomads, groups in Africa (Swahili, [Sobania 2003, 106], Mbuti, Fulani, groups in Guinea-Bissau [Oliver 2003, 67]), Papua New Guinea, and Papua, Indonesia. Round houses are more compact than rectangular houses and have only one main room combining the functions of visiting, cooking, eating, and sleeping. Round houses have one entrance, which fosters Strong Community.

Round compounds, such as in polygamous communities in Africa, have a round house for each wife within a circular compound. The compound also has separate structures for eating, sleeping, cooking, etc. The houses are situated around a courtyard, where daily communal activities take place (Sobania 2003, 106).

The rectangular house is the more common shape as it can easily have additions or alterations (e.g., the traditional Korean L-shaped home) (Clark 2000, 93). Functions such as visiting, cooking, eating, and sleeping are typically divided into separate rooms. Rectangular houses can have more than one entrance and can accommodate Strong or Weak Structure as each room can be for a different person or a different function. A rectangular house can also accommodate Weak Community by allowing people to have their own room or space.

House Structure

A house can have single or multiple structures attached to one another or detached. A house can also be single or multi–leveled or even multi-storied (e.g., apartments). A house can also be for a single family or provide for multiple family housing. Houses with multiple structures or levels provide more options to distinguish status differences such as in the Hierarching Asian home (see Figure 10 below). Strong Community cultures often have one large house with individual sleeping compartments and cooking areas, but have common yards and work areas such as in parts of Latin America (Hugh-Jones 1972, 247) and Southeast Asia (Hakansson 1980, 88).

House Location

The things around a house—geographic features, plants, animals, climate, and neighboring houses—also give the feeling of "home". Differences in any of these areas can make you uncomfortable over a period of time.

A body of water (ocean, lake, river), geographic formations (hill, mountain, valley, plain), or the type of land (sand, rock, coral, fertile soil) can also shape your orientation to life. These major geographic features impact your childhood experience and can result in discomfort when you move to a place with a different geography.

The plants that are common to a particular location become unconsciously familiar and contribute to the feeling of being at home. Pine trees, redwoods and grapevines are common in the hills of Northern California; chaparral, a sturdy bush that grows in drier climates, is more typical of Southern California. In warmer climates palm trees are common, and tropical areas have smaller flowering or fruit bearing trees. Tropical plants bloom more than once a year, and some plants produce fruit up to three times a year. The availability of certain seasonal foods can also make you feel at home.

Certain animals may also give one the feeling of being at home. A US American may miss a pet dog when they go on vacation; others may think of dogs as work animals or food. Jaguars, anaconda snakes, anteaters, and colorful birds are found in Latin America. Lions, elephants, and tigers are typically found in parts of Africa and Asia, while kangaroos, wallabies, and emus are indigenous to Australia.

Sometimes plants and animals of a particular region play an important part in the local worldview beliefs. Flowers often symbolize an area; e.g., tulips in the Netherlands, heather in England, and orchids in parts of Asia. Animals may also take on symbolic meaning (the bald eagle for the United States, the *garuda* bird of Indonesia, the bird of paradise in Papua New Guinea, and the brightly colored *quetzel* in Guatemala). If certain plants and animals were important in your childhood home, your present day home might feel incomplete without them.

Another aspect of a house's location is the climate. People unconsciously adjust to the weather patterns of their home area, as well as the particular house construction appropriate to the area. People in a cold climate feel at home in homes constructed to endure the cold; e.g., an insolated Northern European home with a fireplace. A Pueblo Indian feels at home in dry, hot weather in a traditional home constructed of thick mud, clay, or stone built in layers to minimize sun exposure and maximize cooling. People who live by the ocean feel at home in houses that have a view of the ocean or where they can hear the waves.

In the hot humid tropics, houses are traditionally built up off the ground with tall ceilings, and large overhanging roofs to allow breezes to cool the house. The above ground structure also keeps animals out of the house. In warm climates thin walls allow heat loss. In these homes, there are fewer walls so the air can flow freely. In cooler climates houses are constructed with thicker materials and more walls to retain the heat, or are built in locations that utilize the sun's heat and/or use heating devices.

Population density can make you feel "at home" or "not at home." If your childhood home was in the city, you may feel unsettled living in a rural area as an adult. If your childhood home was in a rural area, you may be unsettled living in the city. There are unconscious stressors in adapting to more or less noise, more or less traffic, and more or fewer people.

House Arrangement

The physical arrangement of a house can make you comfortable or uncomfortable. You may be uncomfortable if the rooms were designed for people who are physically smaller/bigger, shorter/taller, or thinner/wider. You may feel exposed if the walls are constructed out of slats instead of completely covered. You may feel isolated if the walls are completely covered and you are used to partially covered walls. You may feel exposed with half walls if you are used to completely covered walls.

The rooms of a house might also be arranged in an unexpected way: e.g., the bathroom next to the kitchen; the eating/dining room separated from the kitchen; the bedroom in the front of the house rather than the back; a house with one entrance; small windows; sheer curtains; or no bathroom door. You may also not be used to having separate rooms for people of different status.

In a US American home several rooms are often visible from the front door, but some Asian homes open only into the visiting area. The central patio of a Mexican home is visible from the front door, indicating whether anyone is home. The entryway into many Asian homes is built lower than the floor so that people remove their shoes before stepping up into the home.

House Symbolism

A house has its own cultural meaning shaped by the cultural framework of the people who live there. Strong Community cultures (non-Western) consider a house to have a spiritual meaning, while Weak Community cultures (Western) define a house primarily as a material structure. The spiritual meaning of houses includes the fact that both the living and the dead are thought to reside there. Indonesian houses are considered to be alive as the people in it, both living and dead, share their spirits with the house (Waterson 1990, 115).

> The house is a meaningful cultural object. People—builders who envision the end result, dwellers who inhabit and use its space, observers who seek to understand its cultural role— endow the house with meaning according to their culture's worldview and ethos (Rakoff 1977, 85).

Another house with a spiritual meaning is the Hindu *prasada* (seven story mansion) that resembles the Hindu universe with its seven worlds. The foundation is the feet, the upper part is the arms, the walls are the shoulders, the balcony the nose, the windows the eyes, the terrace on the top floor the forehead, and the head is the topmost part (Khambatta 1990, 266).

Hugh-Jones (1972, 246-247) explains that the communal house in Latin America symbolizes the world. The roof represents the sky, the vertical posts the mountains, and the floor the Underworld. The main door of the house is the men's door, representing the mouth where food enters. On both sides of the house are family compartments where food is dispersed. At the opposite side of the entrance is the women's door symbolizing where digested food goes out as human waste.

The Chinese house is understood to be the place where the supernatural force *ch'i* (human spirit, energy, or cosmic breath) lives. The house connects the people in it with the universe. In order for people to live harmoniously in a house, a vertical and horizontal analysis is conducted before construction begins. The vertical aspect represents the link between the universe and the events of daily life; the horizontal dimension represents interpersonal relationships. These relationships are understood through the principle of *yin yang* (complementary opposites). *Yin* is dark, *yang* is light; *yin* is passive, *yang* is active. When these two forces are united, they create harmony. *Yin* represents earth and *yang* represents heaven. Land, houses, the land of the dead, females, and internal things are included in *yin*. Heaven, sun, water, the family, and the land of the living, males, and external things are parts of *yang*. This concept of duality, along with five elements of nature—metal, wood, water, fire, and earth—are used to analyze and harmonize a house. All these cultural concepts are used to determine the appropriateness of a house structure. These concepts are also used to determine the location, construction, layout, and decorations of the individual rooms.

The Chinese worldview also associates the four cardinal directions with a color, an animal, a season, and an element of nature (See Figure 8). North is associated with black, reptiles, winter, and water. East is associated with blue-green, the dragon, spring, and wood. South is associated with red, the phoenix bird, summer, and fire. West is associated with white, the tiger, autumn, and metal. The center is associated with yellow, man, and the earth. The diagonal line that runs from the northeast to the southwest separates *yin* from *yang*— the north and west representing *yin* and the south and the east *yang*. An understanding of the Chinese worldview begins with these classifications (Tuan 1974, 232).

Houses are considered alive if they follow the rules for determining the best (most auspicious) location to build a house, the way the house is constructed, and the materials used (Forshee 2006, 83). You take your own cultural house symbolism with you to another culture and may be surprised or shocked to discover symbolism in another culture that is very different from yours. Going from a materialistic to a spiritualistic view of the house or vice versa leads to many unconscious misunderstandings.

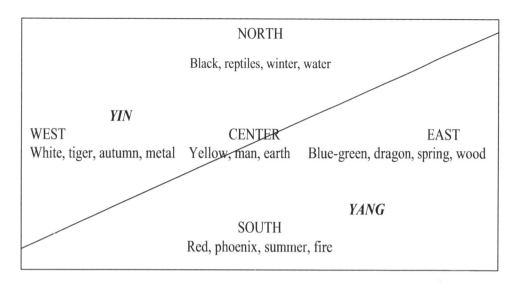

Figure 8: The Chinese Worldview (Tuan 1974, 232)

Structure and Community of Houses

Houses can also be analyzed in terms of Structure and Community. Strong Structure houses have spaces to differentiate status; Weak Structure houses minimize differences. Strong Community houses combine activities (eating, visiting, working, resting); Weak Community separates activities.

Individuating and Institutionalizing homes (e.g., the US American house) focus on the material aspect of the house, and more time and energy are spent on maintaining the physical aspects than on social interaction. The US home is an example of Weak Community, with separate rooms for each function (visiting, eating, working, and resting). The ideal is for each person to have his or her own bedroom. Sometimes spouses even sleep in separate rooms.

Individuating homes focus on the owner's individual preferences such as color, style, kinds of furnishings, how they have fixed up the yard, etc. What you find in one Individuating home will not be the same as in another Individuating home (in contrast with more uniformity in Strong Community homes). What an Individuating person points out are the unique features of his or her house that make it stand out from the others. They do not like their house to be grouped together with others unless it is a comparison that makes them stand out as better than other people.

American homes are also Institutionalizing in that they have to follow building codes and conform to local rules set by an association or city. In order to make changes to an existing house, the house owner needs to apply for the appropriate permit and follow the specific building codes. However, the rules for construction are not the same in every location. They differ within a State as well as between States. It is the responsibility of each person to find out what the local rules are.

Strong Community homes are considered to be living entities. Homes include ancestral shrines and sacred spaces in the home to maintain relationships with the dead. Strong Community homes have more symbolism, while Weak Community homes have a more physical and functional meaning.

Javanese houses are an example of Strong Structure homes. Different roof structures indicate status. Commoners have a simple roof supported by four corner posts. A middle class house has a roof with five ridges that form a hip roof with an extended peak on top. The middle class house also has a verandah. A high-class house has a roof with a tall peak that is at the center of a family compound of other household structures. It also has tiled steps and a verandah (Forshee 2006, 91).

Hierarching and Interrelating homes (e.g., the Asian house and the yurt illustrated in Figures 10-11) focus on the spiritual nature of the home. The home is considered a living entity where past, present, and future family members live. The house itself is sacred as are specific spaces inside the house. The focus is on family interaction rather than the material aspects of the house.

Hierarching homes include areas that respect status, such as a separate eating area for the highest status person or different visiting areas based on status and gender. People with higher status also have better seating arrangements and better food. Family interaction is at the center area of the house.

The layout and use of space in Interrelating homes show equal values for male and female, sacred and secular, and front and back sections of the house. Although the yurt may be physically smaller than other houses, people who live in yurts also utilize the space outside the house for living activities.

The following three house floor plans reflect Individuating (Weak Structure and Weak Community) and Institutionalizing (Strong Structure and Weak Community), Hierarching (Strong Structure and Strong Community), and Interrelating (Weak Structure and Strong Community) types.

Three House Floor Plans

The house floor plan as a microcosm of culture can readily be seen by comparing the shape and arrangement of space in an American home (Figure 9), an Asian home (Figure 10), and a Central Asian yurt (Figure 11). Each floor plan illustrates how the use of space reflects cultural ideals.

An Individuating/Institutionalizing American Home

The typical American home (See Figure 9) is a combination of Individuating and Institutionalizing activities. When purchasing a house, American sellers seek to appeal to the individual choices of buyers. Some houses include a number of options—choice of carpet, windows, and colors—that the seller will make in order to sell the house. Some sellers advertise the specific ways buyers can make the new home suitable to their tastes. At the same time, American houses often have to be built following local rules and regulations. For example, houses can only be built in an area zoned for residential use, not in a business area. In some housing complexes, the houses have to be in line with the rules of that particular complex. However, different complexes have different rules. When a person moves from one location to another, it is up to him or her to find out what the local building regulations are.

When a house is built, the construction company has to follow local and regional building codes. A building permit must be submitted and accepted before any work can begin. Then each phase needs to pass an inspection before the next phase can begin. Work on a house can be delayed if the proper rules are not followed. Even so, there are a number of choices that can be made along the way as to materials, style, and cost.

The suburban American house in Figure 9 is rectangular and is on a lot that is enclosed on three sides. There are six-foot fences on two sides and in the back that separate the house from neighboring houses. The front side is open to the street with a driveway for cars to enter the two-car attached garage. People can enter the house through the garage if it is open. There is a grass lawn in front of the house and a driveway that leads to the front door and the garage. There are three entrances—front, back, and through the garage. Only family and close members use the garage entrance; others use the front entrance. The back entrance goes from the house into the enclosed back yard where there is a covered patio, a pond, and a swimming pool. The house has three bedrooms and two bathrooms, a kitchen, a dining room, and a living room. There are two hallways. One hallway is the entryway and the other provides access to the bedrooms. The attached garage is at the front of the house.

There are a number of houses on the same street that had the same house floor plan. The houses were built in the 1950s. At first the houses were not built close together, but several houses have been built between the original houses. The area was previously rural but now is suburban.

This house was occupied by two generations—parents and children. The parents occupied the master bedroom, which has a private bathroom: the two sons each had their own bedroom and shared the other bathroom. The front door opens into an entryway. On the right side is the kitchen and dining room and on the left are the bedrooms. The living room is to the right of the bedrooms.

When a US American house goes up for sale, the important features are the location, the number of bedrooms, and the number of bathrooms. Buyers are interested in how far the house is from shopping areas, schools, churches, and public transportation or highways. The other selling features are things the buyer can change to reflect his or her individual preference. When the house in Figure 9 was put up for sale, the real estate agent had several fruit trees taken out so that the new owners could decide if they wanted trees and if so, what kind.

Figure 9: An American Home

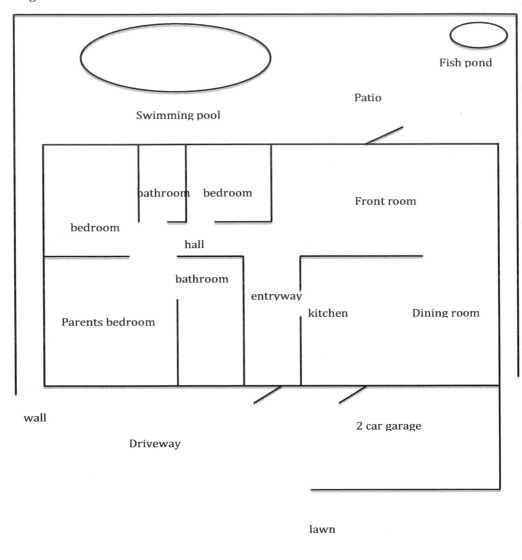

There are little gendered, status/role, or sacred spaces in the American home. The closest concept to sacred space is the sense of privacy. The main status differentiation is that the parents' bedroom is normally the largest bedroom. Although the ideal is for each child to have their own personal space, if there are more children than bedrooms, several boys or several girls would share a bedroom. Individuating people become aware of their perspective when they enter a home from a different culture and listen to themselves talk about how the house is different from their previous house and particularly how it is different from what they like.

Figure 10: An Asian Home

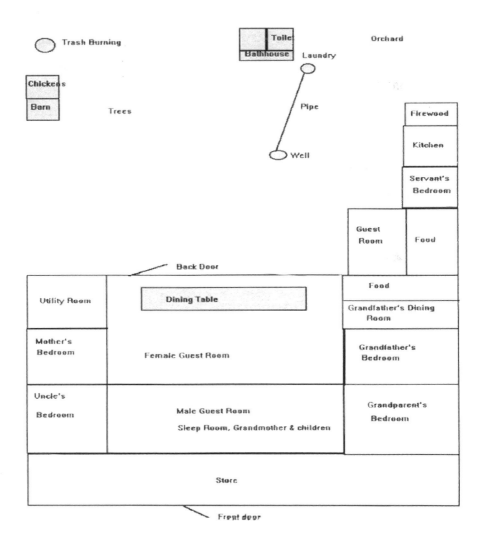

A Hierarching Asian Home

The Asian home is viewed as a living home—the spirits of both the living and the dead ancestors are said to live here. There are two main buildings in the illustrative Asian home (See Figure 10)—the main building and the back building. The main building is rectangular with four bedrooms, two visiting areas, three dining areas, and a utility room. The utility room is a sacred place where family heirlooms and ancestral items are kept. In this particular home there is also a store in the front of the house where food staples are sold. The back building is also rectangular, but smaller than the main building. This building has two rooms—the kitchen and the servant's bedroom. The laundry, bathing area, and toilet are at the back of the property. There is also a barn for the chickens and a garden area to the side of the servant's bedroom. The firewood for cooking is stacked behind the servant's bedroom.

Public and private spaces in this Asian home are determined by gender, status, and role. The grandfather has special areas (bedroom and dining room). The grandmother shares a bedroom with grandfather when she is not sleeping with the grandchildren. Higher status individuals enter through the front door; lower status people go around to the back of the house and do not enter the main house. Males meet in the first visiting area; females visit in the second room. Family members freely use the central spaces inside the house, but the servants stay in their rooms in the back except when serving food or cleaning. The grandfather eats in a separate dining room. Only after he finishes eating do the rest of the family begin to eat. The use of space in this house reflects the Hierarching cultural ideal. This floor plan reinforces the Hierarching cultural ideal of the people who grow up in this home.

Hierarching people become aware of their cultural perspective when they enter a different kind of home and notice that the other home does not give respect of space to people who are older or higher in status or does not have space to interact as a family.

An Interrelating Central Asian Home

The yurt (See Figure 11) as well as the Navajo *hogan* and round houses in Papua New Guinea contrast with most homes in that it is not only round but also has only one room. All household functions take place within the circular space of the home or in the surrounding yard. In round homes, the cultural ideal is not privacy, but doing things together. The round shape of the house facilitates customs that are repetitive, cyclical, and/or complementary. A person enters the only door, which typically faces East, and follows the same direction as the sun in moving through the house.

The yurt is used for hunting trips because it could be easily moved and is made of readily available materials (fur, skin, and sheep wool) covering the wooden frame and is suited to the climate. The yurt is white if it belongs to a tribal chief and gray for others (Abazov 2007, 205).

For many years yurts were used in Central Asia during all seasons except the coldest part of winter when people lived in simple cottages made of sun dried brick (Abazov 2007, 204-206).

The yurt also symbolizes a living human body. The framework is the skeleton, the center is the umbilical cord, and the pockets in the smoke opening are eyes. There is a front and a back. The side lattices are pelvic bones, the bend at the top is the shoulder, and the base of the dome rods is the belly (Shakhanova 1992, 158). The yurt is connected to the universe through the smoke hole at the top. The smoke hole is the place where human spirits connect with supernatural spirits as the smoke rises to the sky.

Figure 11: A Yurt House

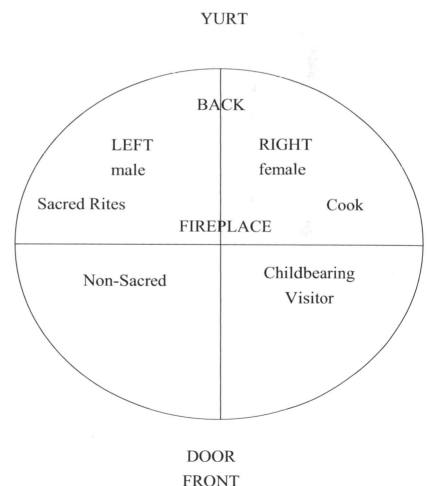

YURT

BACK

LEFT
male

RIGHT
female

Sacred Rites

Cook

FIREPLACE

Non-Sacred

Childbearing
Visitor

DOOR
FRONT

The space inside the yurt is also divided by complementary concepts of sacred and secular as well as female and male. These themes are found in practically every cultural custom, from marriage and building a house to child rearing, cooking, and eating. The left side of the yurt is the male side, where typical male things (axes, arrows, tools, etc.) are placed; the right side is the female side, where typical female things (cooking utensils, bedding, baby things, etc.) are placed. The half closest to the door is the secular half, and the back half is the sacred half, where rituals take place (Shakhanova 1992, 157-183).

The complementary nature of the use of space in the yurt is different from Western homes. Although most Central Asians now live in rectangular buildings (either apartments or individual homes), they still use the yurt for ceremonial occasions and retain customs that originated in the yurt. The complementary use of space reflects the Interrelating cultural ideal. In the same way that culture impacts this house floor plan, the house floor plan reinforces the cultural ideal of the people who grow up in this home.

Interrelating people become aware of their perspective when they enter a home from a different culture and see that the other house does not reflect equality or complementation.

Cultural values influence the physical structure of a home, the typical features of its location, and the house arrangement. Differences in any of these aspects can make people feel uncomfortable, upset, or even distressed.

CBJS and the Home
The longer you have lived in one home the more your level of comfort increases. However, when you move to another house, all of your comfortable ways of doing things have to be adjusted. If you are familiar with the surrounding culture, these adjustments are easier to make. However, when you move to a house in another culture, the adjustments may seem too difficult to overcome. The unsettledness in your home may correspond to your unsettledness in the culture as a whole. At this point your CbJS kicks in, and, depending on your type, you will respond with the normal response of your type.

If you are from a Weak Structure culture, you may get frustrated, upset, or angry when:

- a house is not to your liking—e.g., the construction, building materials, windows, walls, doors, layout, furnishings, and color

- your preferences are not possible due to local rules and regulations

- you were not able to make choices about various features of the house

Your belief in Weak Structure justifies:

- explaining how the construction, building materials, windows, walls, doors, layout, furnishings, color, etc. of houses could be better

- adjusting as many things as you can to your liking

- criticizing the system because it doesn't allow your choices

- trying to find ways to work the system to get the changes you desire

If you are from a Strong Structure culture, you may get frustrated, upset, or angry when:

- a house is not built according to the specifications of your culture

- the layout and allocation of space in the house don't follow the established rules

- the spaces do not allow the categories of your culture to be respected (e.g., more space for higher status, birth order, age, and gender)

- more space is allocated to a lower status person

Your belief in Strong Structure justifies:

- getting angry at the people who do not follow building rules

- seeing that people are punished for not following the rules

- preventing people from making changes to the rules

- being afraid to speak up about not liking the rules you have to follow

If you are from a Weak Community culture, you may get frustrated, upset, or angry when:

- a house isn't divided by function, but by categories such as sacred/secular or male/female

- the larger central area has too many overlapping functions and doesn't give you enough private space

- the house isn't big enough for your needs

Your belief in Weak Community justifies:

- criticizing the house construction and comparing it to your previous house

- ignoring or violating sacred and gender spaces

- not visiting people because their house makes you so uncomfortable

If you are from a Strong Community culture, you may get frustrated, upset, or angry when:

- there is not enough overlapping spaces to foster social interaction

- the main part of the house is not in the center of the house (thus hindering people from socializing there)

- people don't believe it when you say "my house is your house"

- people don't come to your house to visit you

Your belief in Strong Community justifies:

- putting social pressure on people to make their house more sociable

- talking or gossiping about people who don't visit you

- putting pressure on others to use their house for social activities

- unwilling to cause loss of face by saying you don't like something

Your CbJS can distort the image of God in your decision making, beliefs, and emotions regarding your housing.

How a House Distorts the Image of God

When I went to Asia over 30 years ago I did not understand my Individuating cultural practices. I took control of my house and made as many changes as I could to make it comfortable (e.g., adding thick curtains, putting screens on the window, installing an air conditioner, buying new appliances, etc.) according to my preference. I thought making my life more comfortable would enable me to do my work better and be more efficient. I complained about how difficult it was to do everyday chores. I was generally unhappy and made my family and others around me unhappy. I did not understand that my cultural background promoted materialism and consumerism rather than faith and godliness. I was distorting the image of God by using physical things to replace reliance on God in my life. I was not depending on God for comfort and peace. Rather I was relying on physical things to give me comfort. Of course, I didn't find peace and comfort in these material things. I distorted God's image in me through my decision making, my beliefs, and my emotions.

~

EXERCISE

...4A: Describing My Childhood Home

1. What memories do you have of your childhood home?

2. When you moved into a house built according to another culture's standards, what changes did you make?

3. Briefly describe the childhood home you remember in vivid detail, as best you can. Include in your description the house's location, the surrounding geography, its shape, size, structure, entrances, number of stories, and the number of rooms.

~

CULTURE BASED JUDGING SYSTEM QUESTION #3:

HOUSE FLOOR PLANS

Choose the statement that best describes the house floor plan of your childhood home. My home had...[27]

___ 1.   individual rooms for each function (visiting, eating, sleeping, working). If I didn't have my own bedroom, I really wanted to have one.

___ 2.   separate rooms for separate function with rules focusing on the particular function rather than social interaction. I feel uncomfortable if there are no clear rules for the use of each room.

___ 3.   space differentiated hierarchically (age, gender, and status). I feel unsettled if hierarchical distinctions are not observed in the use of space.

___ 4.   equal or complementary use of space. I am uncomfortable in a home that does not have a sense of equality or complementation.

Reflection #5:

House Floor Plan

1. Think about a place that you have moved into. Think about aspects of your home that you changed (and why you changed them) in this new and different place.

2. In what way were the changes you made characteristic of one of the cultural types?

3. Use the following verses to consider how your view of houses can build up the spiritual house of God:

   Exodus 20:17; Joshua 24:15; Psalm 127:1; Proverbs 24:3; Matthew 7:24, 12:25; 1 Corinthians 6:19; Ephesians 2:19-22; 1 Peter 2:4-10

4. Share with someone what God is saying to you and pray for one another.

Exercise

...4B: An Exercise of Reflection and Discussion

With a discussion partner, or on your own, reflect on these topics and how your family approached these issues during your childhood, your family's set of preferences concerning these topics, and what you and your family values today...

1. Construction materials/practices. Essential elements of a house.

2. Building rituals/ceremonies.

3. Decorating a home

4. Importance of owning property. Inheritance of house/land.

Chapter 5

How Childhood Visiting Practices Shape Your CBJS

In the previous chapters you looked at the concept of the image of God and a model of culture to consider your cultural type and how your CbJS can distort the image of God. Then you reviewed your childhood family and your childhood house floor plan. In the next five chapters (6-10) you will use the house floor plan to go room by room to see how your childhood cultural practices shaped your CbJS. You will start with the place or room where visiting with non-family members took place.

Your social interactions with others are first shaped by childhood interactions with family members. Then you are taught other rules for relating to non-family members. You may have been taught to show hospitality to acquaintances, work colleagues, neighbors, and friends of family members but not to strangers, people from different ethnic backgrounds, or people from a different economic background.

Strong Community cultures welcome (or are obligated to welcome) family members, but not non-family members. In other cultures guests are not limited to only family members. Some Strong Community homes welcome guests any time of the day or night, while Strong Structure homes, on the other hand, have regular visiting hours or only pre-arranged visiting times. Some US Americans and urban cultures such as Hong Kong consider it more hospitable to host a meal at a restaurant rather than invite people into their home. Australians consider it inhospitable to not invite a guest into their home for a meal. US Americans prefer to host guests whom they have invited rather than people who drop by uninvited, while other cultures anticipate uninvited guests. US Americans want to know how many guests will come so that they can prepare the amount of food necessary in order to minimize the leftovers, while Asians generally prepare extra food for guests to take food home. Every culture has different expectations for visiting customs and can easily judge others based on their own visiting customs.

In order to better understand differing assumptions of your present day visiting practices, this chapter discusses visiting spaces, visiting activities, the CbJS and visiting, and an example of how visiting practices distort the image of God in the childhood home. These topics will help you recall visiting practices in your childhood home to discover how they impact you today.

A Personal Reflection on Visiting

Adjusting to different visiting practices was a source of much of my overseas stress. I thought people were rude when they came to our house without an invitation. In my childhood home the only uninvited guests were people who were trying to sell something. Door-to-door salesmen had a reputation for being very pushy and so I learned that it was not impolite to treat people rudely who came uninvited.

In addition, I was perplexed at the times people chose to drop by. They often came in the early evening between 5 and 7 pm. That was the time we normally sat down as a family to eat. In my childhood home it would be very rude for someone to drop in during a mealtime. It took a while before I learned that normal visiting hours were in the early evening and that people in the local culture ate after the visiting hours. I'm sure the guests could see that I was not happy that they came when they did, but I didn't understand my reaction to their cultural visiting practices.

I also had a problem understanding why people came to visit. Sometimes they asked for money and other times they did not specifically state what they wanted. That left me wondering why they came. I also did not know when it was appropriate to invite people in or to just talk with them at the front door.

After a lot of stress and wondering about appropriate visiting practices, I realized that my neighbor could answer my questions regarding visiting practices. She told me that many people just wanted to see what a foreigner's house looked like or wanted to ask for money because they considered all foreigners rich. She told me that I could ask them to do some work and then give them money. She explained that I didn't have to give the full amount they requested. Her own practice was to give a standard amount to help with things like funerals even if she did not know the people who died. She felt her gift was contributing to the community. She also explained that it was culturally appropriate to invite guests of the same or higher class inside, but to visit with lower class people outside on the porch.

I appreciated her advice but was still upset that people considered me a rich American because in my mind I was from a lower middle-class American family. However, compared to many people in that country, I was rich. I agreed with her advice to have people work for money because my parents had taught me to work for what I got. However, I thought her advice about treating some people better than others was wrong because it was definitely not biblical.

Visiting Spaces

A comparison of the three house floor plans in the previous chapter reveals cultural differences in regard to visiting spaces. In the American home (Figure 9) visiting takes place in the living room, dining room, and often outside on the patio if the weather is nice. Bedrooms are appropriate visiting space only for young children. In the Hierarching Asian home (Figure 10), a guest from the same social status or higher than the host enters the front door and is escorted to the men's or the women's visiting area. Lower status guests go to the back entrance to speak with the servant. In the Interrelating yurt (Figure 11) visiting takes place in the front half of the house, which is also the secular area.

Some cultures receive guests inside the home, while others receive guests outside in an open area in front of the house as in Java (Forshee 2006, 91). In warmer climates, guests are received on porches or verandahs. Among the New Zealand Maori there is a special outside receiving area called the *marae* next to the community building where the extended family or entire village receives guests (Austin 1990, 229). The film *Whale Rider* (2002) shows Maori hospitality practices with a ritual gift exchange.

In cooler climates guests are received inside the house in the front room, living room, sitting room, parlor, etc. Strong Community Latins entertain guests in the patio or the center of the home where all the social activity takes place. Other urban Latins and Asians entertain guests in the largest room, which might also be a sleeping room.

The Individuating US American home is classified as an "open" home, without high walls and hedges, allowing guests to see in. Visiting space in US America may be any room or space the host or hostess chooses. It can be the front room or living room or an outside area in the backyard as a patio or around the pool. The use of space also reflects the individuality of functions. The focus is on individuality that is reflected in the entertaining pattern.

> The focus on individuality and specialization of function is also reflected in the entertaining pattern...Cocktails are served in one place, the living room; dinner is served in another place, the family room. Depending on the weather, people may visit the 'patio,' an outside place for cooking, eating and relaxing during summer... Obviously, this is a somewhat stereotyped description of how homes are used, but it illustrates how individuality is characteristic of middle-class American homes (Altman and Chemers 1980, 193).

In Strong Structure cultures hospitality spaces may also differ by age and/or gender. Children may be received in a room for children, and adults may be received in another location. There may be a separate room for women and another for men, as well as another room or space for people of lower status. Adults may be received into the house, but children may only be allowed to play in the yard. The French culture uses the dining room as the main area for guests and does not anticipate a guest to enter any of the other rooms, including the kitchen (Carroll 1987, 15). In other Strong Structure homes higher status people sit closer to the front door, while lower status people sit closer to the back door or even outside. The guest may face the inside, while the host faces the door.

The Institutionalizing host/hostess maintains control through the use of space—where guests are or are not allowed to enter. A closed door indicates private space, while an open door indicates public space.

A separate guest room for overnight lodging might be part of Strong Community homes as families regularly anticipate guests to stay for several days. Weak Community homes may not have a separate guest room for overnight lodging.

Visiting Practices

Greetings and leave takings are cultural rituals that begin and end visiting practices. They take place at entrances, the place where the guest moves from public to private space upon arrival or from private to public on departure. Visiting practices take place between these two events.

Greetings

Gates, doors, and thresholds are typical points of entry. In one-entrance homes guests are easily noted, such as in Mexico (Paden 1993, 114-137) and India (Khambatta 1990, 266). In two-entrance homes, friends and family may enter the back door, while acquaintances or strangers come to the front door. In homes with three or more entrances, entrances may be restricted by gender, age, or other categories.

Initial greeting or receiving spaces are smaller than the actual hosting area. A guest may be greeted outside the home and accompanied inside or may be greeted at the entryway. A Jewish custom upon entering and exiting a house includes touching the *mezuzah* symbol[28] on the side of the door to remind the guests of how they should act inside and outside the house. Russians and Kazakhs believe it is bad luck to hand anything across the doorsill. Others believe it is bad luck to step directly on the doorsill because of the spirits that live under it (Altman and Gauvain 1981, 299).

The doorsill is the location of control into a US American home. If the host does not invite a guest to enter, he or she does not wish to interact with the guest. This is especially to regulate interaction with sales persons who are trained to get their foot in the door. Once they get in the door the host is obligated to listen to their sales talk (Altman and Chemers 1980, 190).

When guests approach a home, they may announce their presence by ringing the doorbell, saying "knock knock," clearing their throat, or calling out a greeting. "Good morning/afternoon/evening." "Is anyone home?" or "Have you eaten rice yet?"

Greeting customs also vary from culture to culture. Some people shake hands, others nod or bow, while others embrace or kiss on one or both cheeks. Handshakes also vary from strong to weak shakes, with one or two hands (two hands together or one hand at the side or holding the other arm). The depth of a bow may be determined by status; e.g., lower status bowing lower to higher status (Strong Structure). Kissing

(Strong Community) may be on one cheek, both cheeks, both cheeks plus one, or vary depending on the marital status (two for married, three for single). In some Latin cultures it is appropriate to kiss both men and women as a greeting, while in others it is inappropriate for men to kiss men. Some Strong Community groups in Papua, Indonesia snap each other's knuckles or pull each other's earlobes. Javanese shake hands lightly and then return the right hand to their chest to indicate receiving the guest into their heart (Morrison and Conaway 2006).

When meeting someone for the first time it may be considered polite to state your full name or it may be more appropriate to be introduced by someone who has a closer relationship with a new acquaintance. In Strong Structure cultures it is appropriate to use your title with your family or given name, while in Weak Structure cultures only the first name is used. In Islamic cultures it is not appropriate for a male to greet or touch a woman or vice versa. The oldest person or head of the household might be greeted first or people might expect to be greeted in order of rank and/or by age (Forshee 2006, 89).[29] It may be appropriate for people of the same sex to greet each other but not the opposite sex. Eye contact may or may not be appropriate.

When there is a celebration involving a number of guests, US American men who are seated are traditionally expected to stand up to greet, while US American women stay seated to greet. In many cultures of Indonesia it is impolite to have one's shoulder higher than others' heads. When guests are seated on the floor, the newcomer must stoop lower than others' heads. In Strong Community cultures it is the arriving guest who initiates greetings with everyone who has already arrived.

Leave Taking

In Weak Structure and Weak Community cultures it is not expected to farewell every guest or for every guest to take their leave from the host or other guests.

In Strong Structure cultures leave-taking may be done in ascending order of importance. That is, the highest status people will be given a place of prominence from which to farewell the guests while the other guests file past them to farewell the high status people first. In some Strong Community cultures people will farewell the hosts and then form a line to greet those who are behind them. In Strong Structure cultures it may be polite for men to rise if women leave before others. The custom may be for the man to extend his hand first when greeting a woman or for men to shake hands only with men.

In Strong Community cultures it is important to greet and farewell everyone. The greeting and leave taking may be the same—embrace, hug, kiss, handshake, etc. Hosts are expected to greet and farewell every guest upon arrival and prior to leaving. The hosts accompany the guest to the entryway or outside, even following the guest down the street to whatever mode of transportation he or she has. In some parts of Asia, the closer the friendship, the farther the host will go to farewell guests. The hosts may even watch until the guests are no longer visible.

Visiting Practices

The invitation to visit and the time, frequency, and purpose of visiting also vary from culture to culture. In Weak Community cultures a verbal or written invitation requires a response; in Strong Community the news of an invitation circulates among group members and a response is not required. However, even though an invitee has responded that they are coming, they could also change their mind at the last minute. For a more formal occasion a written invitation follows the oral information and usually arrives the week prior to a big event. However, in Weak Community the invitation normally is sent out two or three months ahead of time. In Weak Community cultures only invited guests are expected to attend; in Strong Community cultures additional uninvited guests, such as friends of the invitees, are also anticipated.

In many cultures it is appropriate to bring a gift, such as flowers, candy, food, drinks, or something from one's garden for the host. In other cultures hosts anticipate reciprocation at a later time.

In regard to the time of visiting, Individuating cultures vary on the stated time for guests to arrive depending on the desire of the host. Institutionalizing cultures expect their invited guests to arrive at the stated time and to arrive on time. Hierarching cultures expect guests to arrive according to status (most important last). Interrelating cultures don't expect the guests to arrive at the stated time. A Strong Structure German colleague once informed our multicultural overseas group that we should not visit or telephone her family from noon to 2:00 pm (12:00 to 14:00), 5:00 pm to 7:00 pm (17:00 to 19:00), and after 9:00 pm (21:00). In Strong Structure Indonesia, guests typically visit between 5:00 pm (17:00) and 7:00 pm (19:00) in the evening, although the hours are not strictly followed, reflecting Strong Community value as well. The indication that visiting hours have begun is that a family opens the front door of their house (it is closed for the afternoon rest time).

In regard to frequency of visiting, in the Individuating United States, some families seldom or never invite guests into their home, while others invite guests on a regular basis. Some invite guests for special occasions; others invite guests for informal gatherings. Institutionalizing hosts specify the time guests may visit and when they should depart, have an orderly schedule of activities, and expect the guests to follow their rules. In Strong Community cultures such as Uzbeki (Zanca 2003, 1-9), the time of visiting is not set ahead of time nor does a guest need an invitation. However, the host begins to prepare for the guests only once they have arrived. According to Carroll (1987, 15), in French homes guests are not as frequent, but friendships are longer lasting than US American friendships. Carroll states that it may take an outsider a while to develop a friendship with the French. The first visit may be a cup of tea and a short visit and later develop into a meal with a longer visit. Visiting in the United States is normally limited to only a meal and rarely for overnight lodging. Hospitality in other cultures may include both, but generally overnight visits are not welcomed for more than three days.[30]

The purpose of visiting practices determines hosting practices as well as the frequency and duration of visiting. Visiting can be done to demonstrate one's individuality (Individuating), to follow rules of politeness with acquaintances (Institutionalizing), to make requests to people of higher status (Hierarching), or to share resources (Interrelating).

Hospitality in the United States is an individual decision. It may be a means of developing friendship or of being hospitable to new people, or it can be primarily a means of presenting a certain image. A typical first question of US Americans is "What do you do for a living?". This question enables visitors to speak about themselves, as well as to provide an opportunity for the hosts to talk about what they do. Although the US American home has been described as an "open" home without high walls and hedges, relationships are not considered as deep as those in other cultures. Visiting may not be so much to develop relationships, but to exhibit one's own interests. For example, a US American host may offer a house tour to point out his or her individuality. This is unusual in many other cultures.

> In preparation for the visit, considerable time and energy will be spent cleaning the home so as to display the image of order, friendliness, and interest in the guests. The visitors will be greeted at the formal front entrance to the home and then ushered into a public room, such as the living room. Very often a tour of the home will follow, with special features of areas and rooms pointed out, especially those that the occupants themselves uniquely introduced. Males will often go along on the tour, but they generally remain in the background, the discussion centering on the females. It is customary in the American family for the female visitor to be especially attentive to various features of the home and to compliment the hostess on unique and clever aspects of the spatial arrangement and decor. If the male is complimented at all, it is usually because of some technical skills he displays, such as wallpapering or carpentry, but everyone acknowledges that such skills were exercised under the guidance and control of the female (Altman and Chemers 1980, 193).

In Strong Community cultures the purpose of visiting is to share or reciprocate resources. In these cultures the family is very important, and the topic of conversation includes information about family members, both immediate and extended. In Central Asia, when a guest received hospitality, he was also expected to reciprocate peace to the host by tying his horse behind the yurt along with his firearms and hunting knives (making it hard to cause harm to the host) (Shakhanova 1992, 174).

In Asia, Strong Community families who live close to each other may spend periods of time throughout the day in each other's homes, but do not invite non-family members to their home. In Australia, grown siblings and their families who live close to each other may cook their evening meals together on a regular basis. Strong Community Middle Easterners and Central Asians are known for their hospitality and go to great lengths to entertain guests whenever they show up. That is, they begin cooking when the guests have arrived and host them long into the night.

In a Strong Community family, hospitality practices include borrowing or lending particular items to develop and maintain relationships. If a family has a fruit tree, they share the fruit with family members, co-workers, and neighbors. When a family has excess food from a special occasion, they do not store it for the next day, but share it with their neighbors, particularly if the neighbors have been inconvenienced (e.g., by the number of guests passing by or parking their cars in front of their houses). When visiting people in Strong Community cultures, guests may bring a gift to show their appreciation for the hospitality they received or may reciprocate the hospitality at some other time.

In Strong Structure cultures, visiting is normally "up-structure," as in Indonesia and Africa (Maranz 2001, 75); that is, lower status people go to the houses of higher status people to network for resources. If an employee has a personal need, he and his family can go to his employer's house to make a formal request. The purpose of the visit might be to ask a favor or to request a particular resource—money, food, etc. In Indonesia it is expected that the guest ask about the host's family and exchange news of acquaintances (Strong Community) before presenting the request. When the host or hostess has addressed the purpose of the visit, light refreshments are served to indicate that the visit is over. Polite guests will not completely finish the food or drink offered to let the host or hostess know they have been sufficiently hosted.

In some Strong Structure Latin cultures, however, it is not appropriate to discuss work or business during a social event. In Strong Community cultures hospitality is a part of a person's family responsibility, and extended family members may drop in and stay for days.

Celebration of rites of passage also offers an opportunity for hospitality. A family may individually decide to have a rite of passage celebration or it may be a regular family custom to gather together to celebrate these times. Rather than one host and hostess, a family or community might join together to host an event. Friends, neighbors, and acquaintances may be invited as well.

CBJS and Visiting

As you have read through the descriptions of different visiting practices, you may recall specific experiences you have had with cultural differences. Perhaps your expectations were not met or you did not meet the expectations of the host culture.

If you identify with a Weak Structure culture, you may get frustrated, upset, or angry when:

- you are told when you can and cannot visit

- you have to give higher class people better seats, better food, better service

- you have to wait for higher status people to arrive before an event begins

- people don't earn your respect but expect to receive respect due to their position

Your belief in Weak Structure justifies:

- complaining about better treatment for higher status people than lower status people

- treating lower status people the same or better than higher status people

- not waiting for higher status people to begin an event

- not showing respect unless you feel a person has earned it

If you identify with a Strong Structure cultural type, you may get frustrated, upset, or angry when:

- your visiting rules are not followed, e.g., guests do not arrive or leave at the appropriate time

- visitors drop in without making prior arrangements

- people don't tell you they are accepting your invitation

- people don't greet using the appropriate titles or greetings

- lower status people are treated better than higher status people

- lower status people do not treat you according to your higher status

Your belief in Strong Structure justifies:

- reprimanding people about not following the visiting rules (appropriate time to arrive and leave, making an appointment before visiting)

- canceling a function if people don't respond to your invitation

- scolding or punishing people who don't use appropriate titles or greetings

- getting angry at people who don't treat people according to their social status

If you identify with a Weak Community culture, you may get frustrated, upset, or angry when:

- you are expected to conform to the group rather than make individual decisions

- everyone has to say what he or she would like to do in order to make a decision

- people can't make a decision on their own

- you are expected to share your resources with others

- someone you invite invites others without asking your permission

Your belief in Weak Community justifies:

- causing people to lose face by criticizing their visiting customs

- considering people weak because they can't make their own decisions

- getting angry at people for trying to make you share your resources

- getting upset with people who invite others without asking your permission

If you identify with a Strong Community culture, you may get frustrated, upset, or angry when:

- people do not want to share their resources or go along with group decisions

- people like to be known for what they do rather than thinking about the reputation of the group

- people get upset that you've invited your friends to come with you to an event

- people criticize you for the way you host an event causing you to lose face

Your belief in Strong Community justifies:
- ostracizing or punishing people who don't share their resources

- gossiping about people who don't reciprocate

- distancing yourself from people who talk only about themselves

Your CbJS about visiting practices can distort the image of God in your decision making, beliefs, and emotions.

How Visiting Practices Distort the Image of God

I did not always consider stress to be an indication of distorting God's image, but now I do. When I am under stress I complain a lot, get angry easily, don't sleep well, and am generally an unpleasant person to be around. When I am stressed I don't exhibit godly characteristics and do not reflect God's image. When I understood that my cultural values led to false beliefs about myself, then I realized how I was distorting God's image.

When I lived overseas I couldn't understand why I was stressed both when I gave things to uninvited visitors as well as when I didn't. No matter what I did, I felt stress. When I was honest, I admitted that my actions and attitudes were not godly, but I didn't understand why they weren't godly. I knew that the local visiting practices were different than mine, but I still thought my way was the right way. My cultural belief justified my anger but didn't help remove it. When I understood that my way and their way were just different cultural ways, I realized that God wanted me to show a godly response towards others and not for them to adjust to my way of doing things. I could, with God's help, change my response to their cultural practices and treat them as people made in God's image.

I learned I needed to focus on the biblical principles of hospitality (Pohl 1999) (see Scripture below) and to break out of my Individuating cultural background and be more hospitable. I also needed to be wise in using hospitality to exemplify the truths of the Gospel to further God's kingdom. When I learned that the host culture had regular times for informal visiting, I was able to change my own schedule to accommodate to the local visiting practices and use the opportunity as a built-in mechanism for showing God's love to the visitors. This perspective helped reduced the stress I experienced with unannounced guests.

When I understood the difference between my culture and the local culture, I realized I had been judging them based on my cultural perspective rather than on biblical truth. I also realized that they could teach me about biblical hospitality and generosity. I needed to be more generous, but also wise in my generosity.

EXERCISE

...5A: Childhood Visiting Practices

1. List as many different greetings and leave-takings as you can remember that you have experienced and describe how you felt using different greetings.

2. Briefly describe a particular experience when you had guests in your childhood home. Who came to your home? How were preparations made? What happened?

Culture Based Judging System Question #4:

Visiting

Choose the statement that best describes your preference concerning visitors. I prefer...[31]

___ 1. only people I have previously invited to visit in my home. I don't like it when people drop in uninvited.

___ 2. people I invite to follow the visiting rules in my home. I do not like people who ignore my rules.

___ 3. following the proper order that respects older or higher status people during visiting. I don't need an individual invitation and I get very embarrassed if I'm served before an older person.

___ 4. to share food and time in my home with my family/community who reciprocate on a regular basis. My community doesn't need an individual invitation. I don't like it when others get more food or when people don't reciprocate.

Reflection #6:

Visiting

1. Think about a recent visiting or hospitality practice you experienced that was different from your childhood home.

2. In what way can the difference be explained by one of the cultural types?

3. Read the following verses about biblical principles of hospitality. How might your understanding of cultural types help you be more biblically hospitable?

   Romans 12: 13; Hebrews 13:2-3; I Peter 4:9-10; 2 John 10; Luke 10:10-11

4. Share with someone what you learned and pray for one another.

EXERCISE

...5B: An Exercise of Reflection and Discussion

Either with a discussion partner or on your own, reflect on these topics and how your family approached these issues during your childhood, your family's set of preferences concerning these topics, and what you and your family values today...

1. Friendship. Kinds of friends. How friends relate to each other. Importance of non-family friends for children/men/women.

2. Communication styles (direct versus indirect).

3. Giving and receiving, borrowing and lending. Limits/kinds of items that may be received/borrowed/given. Responsibility to repay/reciprocate.

4. How people are invited to visit. How people respond to invitations. How guests are expected to act.

Chapter 6
HOW CHILDHOOD EATING PRACTICES SHAPE YOUR CBJS

O ne of the most basic functions of the family is providing food. Food activities involve buying, preparing, and eating the food, and disposing of the leftovers. In order to better understand differing cultural values involved in eating practices, this chapter will look at eating spaces, eating activities, the CbJS and eating, and an example of how eating practices distort the image of God. These topics will help you recall eating practices in your childhood home and discover how they impact you today.

PERSONAL REFLECTION ON EATING PRACTICES

I grew up on a farm and had fresh fruits and vegetables daily. When I went away to college it took a while to adjust to canned fruits and vegetables. Because my mother did all the cooking, I did not learn to cook until I took pre-field training before going overseas. There I learned to cook everything from scratch. I even learned to make things my mother never made, such as bread, pickles, and even catsup.

When I lived in other cultures, I had difficulties adjusting to how much time it took to shop for and prepare food. I missed American food ingredients. Sometimes the local stores carried Western foods and other times they were out for months. I started buying food in case lots, but then the food spoiled because we did not use it up quickly enough. I got impatient when the stores were out of ingredients I used. I criticized the host country for being backward because they couldn't keep up with the consumer market.

When we lived in a local village, we ate whatever was in season. When it was corn season we ate that three times a day—broiled, boiled, or steamed. I got very tired of corn because I was not used to eating the same food all day and so many days in a row.

When we attended social functions on behalf of our organization, we were normally served first and were given better food. I liked the attention I received as a high status person, but I felt I didn't deserve special treatment. I also thought it was wrong and unbiblical that I was treated better than other people.

> *I liked to sample different kinds of food to say that I had tried them, but I didn't always like them. I ate dog meat, various strange fruits, raw insect eggs, fried insects, and a very bland starchy pudding that got stuck in my throat. There were some things I ate that I did not even know what they were.*
>
> *In one community the people told us that if we ate their food we would learn to speak their language. I thought it was an old wives tale, but later realized that people talk when they eat together. I could learn to speak the language if I ate with them every day.*

Eating Spaces

Eating spaces refer to where food is stored, prepared and eaten. In many cultures, after food is harvested it is stored in a separate building, a room in the house, a separate cupboard, or in an outside porch or other outside area. In Spanish speaking countries the food storage room is called a *bodega*, in Indonesia a *gudang*, and in the United States it can be a cupboard, a pantry, or a downstairs cellar.

In many homes food is prepared in a special cooking area or kitchen inside or outside the house. In Weak Structure homes the same room is used for preparing and cooking food, but Strong Structure homes often have more than one space: e.g., a dry and a wet kitchen, a hot or cold kitchen, or a kosher and non-kosher kitchen. These distinctions are based on cultural values about food that require distinct areas for preparing and eating certain foods.

Food may also be eaten in different areas of the house. Individuating US American homes may have a separate place (breakfast nook) for the morning meal, a kitchen table for regular family meals, a formal dining room for special occasions, and an outside area for informal meals. In other homes the same table may be used for all meals, whether in the kitchen or in another room. Some families eat at tables with individual chairs or benches; others eat on a clean surface on the ground while squatting or sitting on the ground or on pillows (Mack and Surina 2005, 130). The eating table may be low (allowing people to sit on the floor), medium height (allowing people to sit on chairs), or high (allowing people to stand while eating). People in Individuating cultures may eat alone in a variety of places—in front of the television, in their car, or at their office desk.

In the American home shown in Chapter 4 (See Figure 9), food is eaten in the dining room at a rectangular table. The mother sits at the end closest to the kitchen and the father at the other end. The children each have their own chair. In the Asian home (See Figure 10), the food is prepared in the back cooking area by the servants. Most of the food is prepared and cooked early in the morning and set on serving tables for family members to eat during the day. There are two serving tables—one next to grandfather's dining room to serve family members and the other next to the guest room to serve the servants and field workers. Grandfather has his own dining room. The rest of the family eats at the dining table in the room next to grandfather's dining room, and the others eat outside in or near the guest room. In the Central Asian yurt (See Figure 11), the food is prepared and eaten in the back right hand section of the house.

EATING ACTIVITIES

Cultures differ in what is considered food, how it is prepared, who prepares it, when and how it is eaten, and what is done with the leftovers.

Defining Food

Food can be anything that can be eaten for nourishment, but cultures differ in what they determine is edible. This means that not all edible things are considered food in every culture. Rather, local availability, history, and cultural beliefs determine what people eat. Some of the more exotic foods people eat are insects and their larvae (ants, flies, dragonflies), various animals (armadillo, bats, rats, snakes), parts of animals (eyes, brains, feet, intestines), tree bark, birds' nests, sea cucumbers, half formed eggs, fermented beans and milk to name a few (Well 2006).

Rice, sweet potatoes, potatoes, taro, beans, yams, couscous, millet, maize, cereals, bread, and tortillas are some of the staple foods around the world. Europeans eat dairy products, but Asians avoid dairy products. Fruit may be eaten as a dessert in Asia, but in the US it is a snack. Others consider fruit to be a food given to birds.

In many countries cakes and sweet breads are served for dessert and only eaten after a main meal, but in the US sweet breads (pancakes, doughnuts, coffee cakes) are also eaten for breakfast. Some counties categorize food according to taste, such as the Chinese five categories (sweet, bitter, sour, salty, or pungent). Chinese, South Asians, and Latin Americans categorize foods as "hot" or "cold" referring to its innate qualities, not to the temperature or the taste. In some cultures certain foods are eaten to cure illnesses or to stabilize the body's humors (Bogumil 2002, 1).

For Individuating US Americans eating is an opportunity to choose what an individual likes to eat; in contrast, for Strong Community Brazilians food enhances social relationships and eating together is a true sign of friendship (Milleret 2003, 83).

How Food is Prepared

In some homes only the mother of the house cooks; in other homes the daughters or female servants do the cooking. Chinese men prepare and cook food, but other cultures forbid men to even enter the cooking area. In some cultures the whole family can be involved in cooking activities.

Meats and vegetables are cut, sliced, chopped, cubed, shredded, etc. and cooked with spices. Food may be cooked in a variety of ways—with oil, (sauté, fry), with heat (roast, grill, broil), or with water (boil, baste, steam). Strong Structure and Individuating cultures use a variety of cooking pots for different foods; Strong Community cultures may use the same pot to cook several dishes.

The Strong Structure British culture has a number of rules defining a "proper" meal including "rules about sequences and combinations of foods, with contrasts in flavor, texture, and temperature" (Mason 2004, 131-132). Social class is important in Ethiopian eating customs (Kiple ad Ornelas 2000, 1336). In Madagascar cooking items are classified by status, with water being the lowest status and milk the highest. A status distinction is also made between cooking over a fire to cooking in a pot (Osseo-Asare 2005, 67). In Hindu cultures food must be prepared by a person from the same caste. That is, a high caste Brahmin must not eat food prepared by a low caste person.

Different fuels are used for cooking, such as electricity, gas, kerosene, firewood, and dung. In the Pacific Islands (e.g., Papua New Guinea, New Zealand, Hawaii) food is sometimes wrapped in banana leaves and cooked in the ground with hot rocks placed on top of the food and water poured over the hot rocks to steam the food. Individuating households typically have a number of specialized appliances for frying, roasting, or slow cooking foods or for cooking different foods (e.g., rice, sandwiches, waffles, eggs, etc.).

People in Weak Community cultures normally use written recipes with fixed amounts of ingredients, but people in Strong Community cultures pass down their recipes orally and adjust the ingredients to taste. Interrelating cultures have complementary rules for how food is to be made, served, and eaten. Kazakhs use seven ingredients to prepare special dishes, traditionally have seven types of food on the table, and serve seven courses for special meals. The oldest and most honored guests receive the best parts of the sheep—head, stomach, and thigh. The eldest man or most honored guest carves the meat and gives the ear to children so that they will listen to their parents (Abazov 2007, 239).

Native Americans believe that they should never own more than they need. Therefore, they are always ready to share their food. This Strong Community sharing of food helps prevent them from starving because it helps balance the social and cosmological order. The Strong Community identity makes it difficult to extend this practice to others who do not belong to their group. Many groups in Africa believe that their lives are intricately tied with the land and its produce. For Ghanaians the yam symbolizes life and eating together during the yam harvest is very important for on-going life (Osseo-Asare 2005, 39).

How Food is Eaten

The way food is served, the rules for eating, the way food is eaten, and the time people eat differ from culture to culture, as does the order in which foods are eaten.

Food may be served on individual plates (as in Weak Community cultures) or on a communal plate (Strong Community). In Africa, family members eat out of a communal bowl, using only their right hand (Osseo-Asare 2005, 39). Having several smaller plates for each person reflects Strong Structure values. Serving plates may vary in size (large, medium, or small) and in shape (round, oval, or square). Plates can be made of fabricated materials (e.g., ceramic, porcelain, china, metal, plastic) or of natural materials (e.g., banana leaves, hollowed out pieces of wood, or gourds).

Food may be eaten with or without utensils. Typical eating instruments are forks, spoons, chopsticks. The size and kind of chopstick varies from culture to culture. Koreans use metal chopsticks, Chinese have longer square wooden chopsticks and Japanese use shorter wooden round pointed chopsticks. Some people eat with a fork, and others use a knife to push food onto a fork. Some people eat with a spoon and use the fork to put food into the spoon. Others use pieces of bread to scoop food from a communal plate. Russians use teaspoons to eat desserts (Mack 2005, 121), but US Americans normally use forks to eat cake, pie, and other baked goods. Interrelating Central Asians eat only with their right hand and not with their left hands (Mack 2005, 129).

Individuating US Americans are accustomed to eating off individual plates with separate areas for different kinds of food. Strong Community cultures tend to prefer one main dish such as vegetables and cooked meat mixed together, while Strong Structure cultures prefer to have vegetables and meat served separately with a number of side dishes. Indonesians eat out of a bowl-like plate with meat and vegetables placed on top of a base of rice.

When eating from a communal platter, people in Strong Community cultures only eat the food immediately in front of them. It is impolite to reach across the platter to get some delicious item on the other side. However, a good hostess pushes choice pieces of meat or vegetables for others to reach.

Strong Structure cultures serve food in courses; Weak Structure cultures serve the food all at once. Weak Community cultures have the food served up in larger serving bowls and individuals help themselves, but in Interrelating cultures the mother can divide up the food on everyone's plate before it is served so that everyone gets an equal amount (e.g., Australia and Mongolia) or the food is served on a communal plate from which all can eat (e.g., Morocco and other Arabic speaking countries).

People in some cultures have a drink before their meal, others have a drink with their meal, and still others do not drink until after the meal is finished. Water may be an appropriate drink in some cultures, but tea or wine is appropriate in others. In Russian,

Chinese, and other Strong Community cultures, it is customary to toast using wine or other local alcoholic drinks. These toasts provide an opportunity for community members to mention virtues of other people and to reinforce social relations.

In many cultures a meal is not complete without tea. Tea may be served at the beginning of the meal and between each course. The role of the hostess is to keep the teacup or tea bowl filled. It may not be necessary to empty the cup before it is refilled. In fact, it may be polite to leave some tea in the bottom of the cup. In Individuating cultures it is not impolite to empty one's cup and ask for a refill. It is also important for the host to have a good selection of drinks.

In Strong Community cultures it is very important for family members to eat together. However, in Weak Community United States, the busy schedules of family members make it difficult to eat a meal together on a regular basis. In Strong Structure Japan, the father does not typically eat with the family due to his long work hours. However, a plate of food is served and set aside before the rest of the family is served (Askenazi 2003, 118). In Central Asia, it is impolite to begin eating before the eldest person or the guest starts eating (Mack 2005, 129).

In Strong Structure Great Britain different times of eating, different foods, and names for meals reflect social status, age, and geographical location (Mason 2004, 130), and inStrong Structure Bali it is not appropriate for people from different social levels or castes to eat together (Forshee 2006, 89).

The time of eating also varies from culture to culture. Some cultures eat three or four times a day (Forshee 2006, 131)[32]; others eat only twice a day (Alcock 2007, 182-183)[33]; and some have one large meal a day (Kiple and Ornelas 2000, 1336). Others have snacks between regular meals, such as at a coffee break or teatime (morning and afternoon). Some people eat at the same time every day; others eat at different times depending on their work schedule or other activities. The morning meal may be eaten early or mid-morning. The noon meal may be eaten around noon or until 2:00 p.m. (14:00). The evening meal may be at 5:00 p.m. (17:00) or as late as 7:00 p.m. or 8:00 p.m. (19:00 or 20:00). The larger meal may be at midday or may be in the evening. Historically, the time of eating depended on the family's work schedule. In hot climates outdoor workers eat a smaller meal at midday to aid in digestion (Alcock 2007, 181). The length of meals is longer in Strong Community as it is considered a time to socialize, as in Mexico (Standish 2004, 74).

Meals may also be a time of noisy socialization or of quiet eating. According to Forshee, the Balinese eat quietly and quickly so that their mouths are not opened for a long period of time to reduce the possibility of evil spirits entering (Forshee 2006, 45).

In Interrelating cultures such as the Maasai (Africa) the food is evenly divided between two groups. For special celebrations, an ox is cut up so that there are two equal pieces of each cut. The two pieces are distributed equally to each paired group—elders and their wives, boys and elders, girls and elders' wives, etc. (Sobania 2003, 122).

Leftover Food

The cultural value of food determines what happens to leftover food. In Weak Community cultures food can be stored for a following day or thrown away; it is seldom shared with others. In Strong Structure cultures the taste of food may be thought to lose its flavor after the first day. Therefore, it is thrown out after the first day. In Strong Community cultures families may cook more food than they can eat in order to share with others.

Cultures who have a history of not having enough food tend to treat food as special or sacred and save it for the following days. After centuries of hardship in Russia, people consider bread to be sacred and believe it should not be thrown away. It is better to make croutons or eat stale bread than to waste it (Mack 2005, 119). Bread can also be given to others who don't have enough food. In Hierarching families the oldest adults eat first, then the rest of the family, and household employees eat the leftovers. If there are more leftovers than a family can eat, they give it to their neighbors. Other people use leftovers to make the next day's meal, as in Tunisia (Heine 2004, 114).

CBJS AND EATING

Because food is so important in everyday life, your CbJS is probably the most active when you encounter cultural differences with eating practices.

If you are from a Weak Structure culture, you may get frustrated, upset, or angry when:

- you can't serve yourself, choose the food you like, eat the amount of food you want, or eat when you want to

- you are given an eating utensil you don't normally use

- people receive better food and are served first because of their status

- you have to wait to be served because you are not high status

- you are criticized for being wasteful if you throw leftovers away

- other people think making your own decisions for eating practices is wrong

If you are from a Weak Structure culture, you may get frustrated, upset, or angry when:

- helping yourself to the food you want and choosing your preferred eating utensil

- complaining about different food practices

- not waiting for higher status people to be served first

- throwing away leftovers

If you are from a Strong Structure culture, you may get frustrated, upset, or angry when:

- better food is not served to the elders, males, or higher status people

- food isn't made according to the proper categories (hot and cold, kosher and non-kosher, sweet and savory)

- higher status people aren't given better seating or are expected to serve themselves

- higher status people are seated next to lower status people

- rules about eating are not followed

Your belief in Strong Structure justifies:

- getting angry at people who do not treat higher status people better

- not eating food that has not been prepared properly

- scolding or punishing people who don't follow the rules

If you are from a Weak Community culture you may get frustrated, upset, or angry when:

- you have to wait for others to arrive before you can eat

- the hostess keeps refilling your plate or cup without asking

- you are expected to share a communal plate

- everyone eats food straight from the main serving dish

- you are expected to share your leftovers with the guests

Your belief in Weak Community justifies:

- starting to eat before others arrive

- refusing to eat from a communal plate or main serving dish

- taking food from a communal plate and putting it on a plate to eat by yourself

- getting angry at people who invite their friends to your house without asking you first

- storing leftovers for your own future use

If you are from a Strong Community culture you may get frustrated, upset, or angry when:

- people eat first without waiting for the others

- people don't like the food that is served

- people fill their plates and do not consider whether there is enough to go around

- someone expects to be given better food than others

- people throw away leftover food rather than giving it away

Your belief in Strong Community justifies:

- ostracizing people who do not wait for others to eat, say they don't like the food, or take more than others

- gossiping about people who don't share food

- not sharing with people who do not reciprocate

Your CbJS about eating practices can distort the image of God in your decision making, beliefs, and emotions.

How Eating Practices Distort the Image of God

In reflecting on my eating experiences, I realized how much my own culture shaped my ideals. My responses to different foods and different eating practices did not reflect the image of God, but revealed my CbJS at work.

When I was overseas I was proud of myself for being able to try different foods. However, when I didn't like a particular food, I found myself doing everything I could to not eat it. I also complained when the stores were out of a particular food item I preferred. I judged the country and the people as being backward and the next time the food was available I bought a whole case and hoarded it. When we lived in a more remote area I was very upset when I was served the same food three times a day as I was used to having variety of food at every meal.

When I looked into the Scriptures listed below, God convicted me of judging people when I didn't have a choice of food and when I prioritized food over people. I began to realize how my US American Individuating preference for only eating food I liked made me judgmental of others when I wasn't able to choose or get the types of food I liked. I also realized how much my individuality created a barrier with others who ate different food. I needed to follow the wisdom of the proverb about learning another language by eating food with my hosts. I also needed to understand that eating food was one way of showing my acceptance of others. I was distorting the image of God in me in my beliefs, decision making, and emotions.

Exercise

...6A: Childhood Eating Practices

1. List different foods you have eaten.

2. Briefly describe a particular meal or eating experience in your childhood home.

3. Did your family socialize during meals? If so, why and concerning what topics?

Culture Based Judging System Question #5:

Eating

Choose the statement that best describes your preference concerning eating practices. I prefer...

__1. to choose the food I eat, how I eat it, and the time I eat it. I get upset when others make that decision for me.

__2. to eat food that is prepared and served according to the proper way. I don't like to eat just anything.

__3. having the oldest or most important people served first. I get embarrassed if I am served before older people.

__4. to share food equally with my family and friends (but not with strangers or outsiders). I get upset when it looks like the food will not be shared equally.

⌐⌐

Reflection #7:

Eating

1. Think about a memorable situation involving different food and eating practices.

2. In what way does your response to the difference reflect one of the cultural types?

3. Read the following verses about food and eating practices and consider how your understanding of cultural types enables you respond to different food practices in a more biblical manner:

   Luke 12:22-25; Acts 6:1-7, 10:9-15; Romans 14:1-3, 14; 1 Corinthians 10:23; Galatians 2:11-13; Colossians 2:16

4. Share with someone what God is saying to you. Pray for one another.

⌐⌐

Exercise

...6B: An Exercise of Reflection and Discussion

Either with a discussion partner or on your own, reflect on these topics and how your family approached these issues during your childhood, your family's set of preferences concerning these topics, and what you and your family values today...

1. Eating manners.

2. Significant ingredients, recipes, and menus. Categories of foods. Essential elements in a meal/daily diet.

3. Special foods/meals for special occasions. Value of efficiency, freshness, cost, etc.

Chapter 7

HOW CHILDHOOD WORKING PRACTICES SHAPE YOUR CBJS

T he everyday activities in the childhood home provide food, shelter, and protection. When parents do these everyday activities, they unconsciously model cultural work ideals for their children. They also give verbal instructions on how to work. Depending on the kind and degree of supervision, children may also learn particular attitudes towards work. In many cases present day work activities reflect these childhood work experiences.

Weak Structure and Weak Community (US American) parents tend to model an independent work style, while Strong Community cultures (Japanese) model working hard in order to not bring shame on the family name. Institutionalizing parents train their children to follow the family rules, while Interrelating cultures train their children to work together to share resources equally.

In order to better understand differing assumptions about your present day work practices, this chapter discusses workspaces, types of work systems, work activities, the CbJS and work, and an example of how work practices distort the image of God in the childhood home. These topics will help you recall work practices in your childhood home to discover how they impact you today.

PERSONAL REFLECTION ON WORKING PRACTICES

When I grew up a normal week for work was eight hours a day five days a week or forty hours a week. When I first went overseas, my father asked me if I worked 8 hours a day for the mission agency. He wanted to make sure I fulfilled my work responsibilities. From time to time I remembered what he said and tried to do my best to make sure I worked 8 hours a day. However, after I got married and had children, I was not able to work 8 hours a day on group assignments and that caused me stress because housework often took more time than I anticipated.

I worked in one country overseas where they even worked six-days in a week. At first I thought that was really crazy. Then I found out that the offices were only open from 8:00 am to 2:00 pm and then closed for the rest of the day. On Fridays and Saturdays offices closed by noon. I thought they could be more efficient by working only five days a week and having two days off.

Another work related difficulty I experienced was supervising household workers. I expected I would give instructions only once for each task but found I had to keep repeating myself to get the desired results and even that didn't always work. I also ended up handling personal problems between workers, attending to their medical needs, paying for school bills, and arranging for their time off. It was almost a full-time job keeping on top of the household workers and their personal needs. On top of that, they called me "mother," even though I wasn't that much older than they were!

When I was overseas I thought the local office workers socialized too much on the job and avoided doing work. They were believers, so I thought they should work according to what I considered God's work standard. I would walk around the office and ask various ones jokingly if they were getting their work done hoping to put pressure on them to do more work. They seemed to enjoy the social interaction. As a result they nicknamed me, "Mrs. Policewoman."

Another situation in the overseas workplace really got me upset. One of the employees asked for time off to go to his father's funeral. At first I understood the need to take time off work, but when he asked a second and third time in the same year, I couldn't believe he would lie and not feel guilty. I didn't realize that a person's uncles were also called father.

I didn't realize how my childhood work experiences impacted me until I revisited my childhood home. Because my parents were Japanese American they were put in a relocation camp during World War II and they had to move several times. They had to work extra hard each time they started over. My parents wanted things to be different for their children so they taught us to be diligent and to work hard. I often judged others because they did not seem to be working as hard as I was or because they had different work practices.

WORKING SPACES

In the childhood home, workspaces may be inside or outside the home. Outside work may include keeping the yard clean and doing gardening. Work inside the home may include cleaning, preparing food, caring for children, etc. If the home has separate rooms for different activities, guests may be entertained in the living room (front room, parlor, etc.), food may be prepared in the kitchen, food may be eaten in the dining room, clothes may be washed in the laundry area, bodies may be cleaned in the bathroom, and cleaning may be necessary in all the rooms. If the home has multiple uses of space, a number of those activities might occur in the same place (visiting, eating, sleeping in one room; bathing and toilet in another).

The places you worked in your childhood home may shape your present day feelings towards work. If you worked outdoors in your childhood, you may prefer to work outdoors today. If you did certain work in a specified room, you may prefer following the same pattern as an adult. If you have to work in a different type of space than your childhood, you might be uncomfortable.

In the Individuating American home (See Figure 9) work normally corresponds to the function of the room. The kitchen is for preparing food, the dining room for eating, the laundry for washing clothes, the bathroom for washing bodies, etc. In the Hierarching Asian home (see Figure 10) visiting spaces are assigned by status and gender, and some activities take place in the same room. Guests of the same or higher status are received in the main house. Lower status guests are received in the back area. Eating spaces are also assigned by status. Grandfather has his own dining room, the immediate family eats in another room, and the household staff eats in the room at the back of the main house. Grandfather has his own bedroom, the parents and siblings have their own bedroom, and grandmother sleeps with the grandchildren in the male visiting room. The laundry area, garden, and animal areas are in the back. Hierarching Japanese and Korean homes have fewer rooms but use the same space for different functions (visiting/eating/sleeping). The Interrelating yurt (see Figure 11) is divided by work/activity spaces. The front half of the home is secular space where secular activities such as visiting take place; the back area, where rites of passage take place, is considered sacred. The left side is the place where male activities take place, and the right side is the place where female activities, such as food preparation and childbearing, take place.

Types of Work Systems

The economic system of a culture influences the work habits in the home. There are two basic types of work systems based on the kind of exchange—unequal or equal. The kinship system is an unequal work system based on relationships; the consumer system is an equal work system based on the cost and sales of goods and services. The kinship system is a reciprocal sharing of resources; consumerism is an exchange of equal valued items. That is, each item or service is given a monetary value established according to a standard wage. The item or service is then acquired by an exchange of money normally validated with a written document (i.e., a receipt). Because the exchange is equal, there is no need for an ongoing relationship. In a kinship system, however, items and services are not given a monetary value nor do they need a document to validate the exchange. The items and/or services exchanged can be repaid at a later date and in another manner. Services can also be exchanged for goods and vice versa. Kinship cultures may also be influenced by consumerism. Strong Community cultures tend to use the kinship system, while Weak Community cultures tend to use a consumer system.

An example of the kinship work system in Indonesia is called *gotong royong* (mutual aid) in which the community comes together to build a house, clear a garden, or harvest a crop. The host feeds the workers, but everyone joins in the work together. Each person can request help from the community on a rotating basis. In this way everyone gets basic tasks completed without having to pay for individual labor. The focus is not on individual production of labor, but on the event that brings the community together and fosters on-going relationships. "Barn raising" in early US America and community service days in Australia are similar.

Strong Community cultures have a rotating credit system whereby group members contribute a certain amount for each meeting and one person can take the full amount for a personal need. In this way the community members support each other (e.g., Africa, Asia, Caribbean).

An unequal exchange system allows and encourages negotiation or bargaining for costs or services. In a typical bargaining exchange the seller states a price and expects the buyer to suggest a lower price. However, the exchange also includes a social dimension fostering a social relationship. There may be several similar exchanges to arrive at a price acceptable to both the buyer and the seller. The buyer does not engage in an exchange unless he or she intends to buy the item. In this way social relationships are fostered. A relationship is maintained to ensure continued good prices for the buyer and regular sales for the seller. Because the kinship based economic system is based on a relationship, there is no need to document purchases. In fact, asking for a receipt may be interpreted as a lack of trust on the part of the buyer.

Underlying the kinship system is the belief that there is a limited amount of goods available. Therefore, family members take responsibility for each other and resources are pooled. Although extended family members in an urban setting may have different jobs, they may all bring their wages to the family head. He decides, either individually or in consultation with family members, how to spend the family money. This financial pooling may occur even if family members do not live in the same house. Reciprocity and care for one another is built into the kinship system.

Underlying the consumer work system is the belief that there is an unlimited amount of goods available. Therefore, the consumer work system is based on profits. A manufacturer looks for less expensive raw materials and ways to lower production costs in order to increase profits. The profit is then used to buy more raw materials to make more goods to sell. This work system is measured by the cost of materials, the production costs, and sales. The wage for each person involved in the process goes into the cost. This system encourages individual competition rather than cooperation among individuals or family members. Consumers believe it is up to each person to take advantage of lower prices.

In Weak Community consumer cultures individual work is given a value based on the ratio of cost to sales. A person's work is given a value reflected in his or her salary. Once an equal exchange has been made (i.e. people receive their salary for their work), the exchange is complete. Social responsibility is not a part of the consumer system. If Weak Community people receive a gift that they did not work for, they complete the exchange by saying "thank you." There is no further need for reciprocation.

The equal exchange system does not allow for bargaining and is not based on maintaining social relationships. Prices are fixed and sellers can feel insulted if they are asked to give a lower price as they believe it is their right to set the price. In this work system people accumulate commodities or perform services individually rather than developing reciprocity or maintaining social relationships. The bottom line is to insure that a profit is always made; that is, the cost of producing an item needs to be below the selling price.

In the consumer work system, unlike the kinship system, people do not pool resources. A husband and a wife may even have separate banking accounts and make individual decisions regarding their own money. Paying for a commodity or service does not necessitate an on-going obligation for social interaction. Because there is no social validation of an exchange, it is important to document expenditures to verify purchases. A written receipt also enables the purchaser to return an item or exchange it for another item.

There are particular assumptions underlying each system of production. The kinship system assumes individuals do not operate in isolation, but are a part of the family community. Each family community works together and shares its resources to fulfill its basic needs. The consumer system assumes each person operates individually and takes care of the nuclear family expenses and, therefore, is not responsible for others, including other family members. Although parents provide for children when they are little, they expect their children to learn to take care of themselves when they leave the home (around 18 years of age).

People from a kinship economic system (Strong Community) extend the definition of family to neighbors, church family, co-workers, etc. They are disappointed if others from these groups do not share their resources or are unwilling to accept resources from others. People from a consumer economic system (Weak Community) get upset when others expect them to share their own personal resources. The consumer/kinship difference of work values is a major source of conflict in present day mission groups. When foreign workers from consumer cultures expect the consumer work standard to be the norm in a kinship society, it fosters much misunderstanding. For example, it is important for consumers to get a good price. Therefore, they will go to several sellers to compare prices before choosing a seller. When they don't return to the same seller, the seller thinks he or she might have done something wrong. Additionally most foreign workers are volunteers and must find their own sources of funding, so they prioritize low prices over relationships. Understanding the different underlying assumptions of the two economic systems can shed light on present day misunderstandings in multicultural work teams.

In Strong Community cultures interpersonal relationships are developed in the workplace, but in Weak Community cultures interpersonal relations are not generally encouraged in the workplace. Therefore, interpersonal conflicts in the workplace are not addressed in the same way. In Weak Community, people are expected to keep their personal problems from affecting their work; in Strong Community cultures personal problems are a concern of the whole group. In Strong Community cultures interpersonal relationship problems are viewed as a responsibility of the workplace community; in Weak Community cultures these problems are the responsibility of the individuals involved or of the person's supervisor if it effects a person ability to get work done.

Work Activities

Each cultural type has a different ideal that influences how work activities are viewed and carried out.

In the Individuating cultural type (Weak Structure and Weak Community) work is viewed individually because consumer values shape work practices. Individualists are responsible for their own work and do not take responsibility for the work of others. People from Individuating cultures prefer to have a choice in the kind of work they do rather than being told what to do. From an early age (2 or 3 years of age), US American Individuating children are trained to make choices regarding the clothes, food, and activities they prefer, as well as how to spend their money. Parents learn what their child likes and does not like and cater to the child's preference. For example, if their child likes a particular brand or kind of toy or color of style of clothes, they will get that for the child. Individuating children may also receive money for work or may regularly receive a certain amount of money so that they learn how to make decisions about money. Some Individuating children may be taught how to use money wisely, but many are allowed to decide on their own. Children who are raised in Individuating cultures get frustrated when they do not have individual choice or are expected to share.

The Institutionalizing cultural (Strong Structure and Weak Community) family has clear role distinctions for father, mother, and children according to cultural categories (age, gender, birth order, etc.). The ideal is top down authority supported by closely enforced work rules and regulations. Parents take responsibility for their own children; other members of the extended family do not interfere with parental decisions. Children are taught rules and skills intended to enable them to live independently from their parents. Children who are raised in a Strong Structure culture get frustrated when there are not clear guidelines for doing work. They also get upset when they do not get paid more than others for higher status work, or when others do not work as well but receive the same wage. For Institutionalizing people work is considered more important than people.

In the Hierarching cultural type (Strong Structure and Strong Community) everyone has a distinct place in the social order, and that order is diligently maintained. The father or oldest male is the natural authoritative head. The mother's role is subordinated to or coordinated with the father's role in the division of labor. Gender and age are also often differentiating factors in the family hierarchy. Hierarching families have strictly prescribed social roles that distinguish each person's place in society. Everyone knows his or her place and fulfills the assigned role in order to have a well-ordered society. The belief is that work does not get done appropriately unless everyone does his or her part. The mother oversees work in the home and assigns various tasks to the servants and children. She normally does not perform all the tasks herself. If one person does not do his or her part, this can bring shame on the family or on the group as a whole. Therefore, the family as a whole will make sure that the servants and children do their work. If not, they will be scolded or punished in some way. In Hierarching cultures the main focus is on the family/group as a whole rather than the work.

In the Interrelating cultural type (Weak Structure and Strong Community) the focus is on cooperating to get work done. Helping one another is the ideal, and family members and communities come together to help one another; e.g., get dressed, eat, bathe, shop, do dishes, wash clothes, repair a roof, clear a field for planting. If people help others, they expect to receive help when they have a need. In this cultural type resources are often pooled. Reciprocity is important to maintain equity. Those who do not share equally will be criticized, and social pressure will be exerted to cause them to conform.

CBJS AND WORK
In a multicultural work team you will probably become aware of your CbJS in your everyday work environment and in social interactions when differences arise between group members.

If you are from a Weak Structure culture, you may get frustrated, upset, or angry when:

- the work schedule is not flexible enough for your needs or preferences
- you are not given a choice of work assignments
- you are not allowed to be creative or innovative in your work
- you have to follow work rules and regulations even though they keep changing
- you can't figure out how the system works
- people do not ask your advice or your opinion

Your belief in Weak Structure justifies:

- following your own preferred work schedule

- criticizing work practices that differ from yours

- getting upset when no one asks for your advice or opinion

- trying to get others to do jobs you don't like to do

- rationalizing your work decisions

If you are from a Strong Structure family, you may get frustrated, upset, or angry when:

- the work rules or expectations are not clear

- people don't follow the work rules

- people come to work late or leave early

- people read the newspaper at their desk or chat frequently with co-workers

- authority figures are not authoritarian enough

- authority figures ask your advice

Your belief in Strong Structure justifies:

- identifying people who do not follow the rules and seeing they are punished

- taking advantage of extra benefits that come with your higher position

- preventing people from getting ahead who might be suitable for your position

If you are from a Weak Community family, you may get frustrated, upset, or angry when:

- you have to work on a team rather then doing your own work

- co-workers share their personal problems with you or expect you to help them with a personal need that they have

- people invite you to attend a celebration (e.g., an anniversary, a welcome or farewell party) during work hours

- you are pressured to take time off from work to see sick family members

Your belief in Weak Community justifies:

- organizing the team to do individual tasks rather than teamwork

- not listening to people's personal problems or being willing to help

- prioritizing work over family and friends

- not visiting sick family members even though others told you to

If you are from a Strong Community family, you may get frustrated, upset, or angry when:

- you are expected to work alone

- your co-workers don't take responsibility for you or don't make sure you have what you need to do your job

- people criticize the group's work practices

- co-workers don't seem interested in joining your family celebrations or don't invite you to their family celebrations

- co-workers don't take time off to visit a sick relative or dying family member

- you conform to others work practices but harbor bad feelings about it

Your belief in Strong Community justifies:

- disciplining or ostracizing people who don't demonstrate group loyalty

- gossiping about those who don't conform to group standards

- demoting those who don't uphold the group's reputation

Your CbJS can distort the image of God in your decision making, beliefs, and emotions about working practices.

How Working Practices Distort the Image of God

My greatest cultural discovery in relation to work practices was realizing that I defined work as an 8-hour per day job that I got paid for. I had not realized how much my father's instructions and the Western work system shaped my definition of work. I thought my father (and God) was only pleased with me if I did at least 8 hours of work a day (excluding housework). In line with the Asian American side of my upbringing, I felt it was wrong to express my feelings outwardly, even though I harbored strong negative feelings inside.

When I wasn't able to put in an 8-hour day for my organization, I blamed the household employees for all the things that required my time. I justified my negative feelings because I thought I had the right beliefs in regard to work. When I had more work than I could do, I would try to get other women to take more responsibility for some of the things I had agreed to do. When they didn't take my offer, I got upset with them. I particularly judged women who didn't have a full-time office job. Even though they were mothers of young children, I thought they would want to do something.

When I looked into Scripture, I could not justify my beliefs about work. There was no distinction in Scripture between paid work and unpaid housework. Instead I was to rejoice in everything. Now I realize that I was projecting my own work ethic on other women rather than having an attitude that God would want me to have. I justified my anger towards them because I thought God would be angry with them for not working more. I didn't realize that my work practices followed cultural values and that my responses to different work practices did not honor God. I needed to ask God to forgive my false beliefs and to ask others to forgive my actions in order to restore God's image. I realized that I had distorted God's image in me through my decision making, beliefs, and emotions.

Exercise

...7A: Childhood Working Practices

1. Briefly describe a particular chore or work experience in your childhood home.

2. How many hours a week do you presently spend working? _____

3. How do you distinguish your work from other activities you do at home?

4. Explain if you think you should spend more or less time working than you do.

Reflection #8:

Working

1. Reflect on how work in your childhood home shaped your cultural definition of work and how that impacts a challenging work situation you have experienced.

2. Read the following verses about work and consider what you know about how work is different in the cultural types. How can this knowledge enable you to use these differences to demonstrate unity in the Body of Christ?

   Exodus 23:12: Ecclesiastes 5:19; John 6:27; 1 Corinthians 3:13; Colossians 3:23-24; Titus 3:14; 2 Thessalonians 3:6-11

4. Share with someone what God is saying to you. Pray for one another.

EXERCISE

...7B: An Exercise of Reflection and Discussion

Either with a discussion partner or on your own, reflect on these topics and how your family approached these issues during your childhood, your family's set of preferences concerning these topics, and what you and your family values today...

1. Jobs: types, responsibilities, cultural values

2. Management styles. Opportunity/process for advancement.

3. Employee relations: with superiors, with co-workers

4. Work styles: teamwork, schedule, poor/superior performance

5. Are holidays viewed primarily as work breaks or as celebrations of annual cycles

6. Borrowing and lending items from the company or items from co-workers

Chapter 8

HOW CHILDHOOD RESTING PRACTICES SHAPE YOUR CBJS

Rest is part of the everyday rhythm that enables household activities to take place. Rest can be defined in a number of ways, including sleeping at night and resting during the day. The lack of sufficient rest can affect a person's ability to carry out everyday activities as well as to develop deep interpersonal relationships.

For those cultures where work is a primary focus, rest is defined as everything that isn't work. In other cultures rest and work are a part of everyday life. Weak Community cultures make a distinction between physical, emotional, and spiritual rest; Strong Community cultures consider all three together. Weak Community cultures focus on work, so physical rest is primarily needed to improve or enhance the ability to work. However, when individuals choose to work in order to be able to enjoy leisure activities (such as entertainment, sports, or other activities), they often get less sleep.

In order to better understand differing assumptions of your present day resting practices, this chapter discusses resting spaces, resting activities, the CbJS and resting, and an example of how resting practices distort the image of God in the childhood home. These topics will help you recall resting practices in your childhood home to discover how they impact you today.

A PERSONAL REFLECTION ON RESTING

When I was in Latin America, I thought people were lazy when they took a rest in the middle of the afternoon every day. I thought it was okay to take a rest once in a while, but taking a rest every day seemed very unnecessary. Not only did people rest, but the stores and offices were also closed. I thought they must not care about making money otherwise they would be open all day. When people sleep in the afternoons, they also stay up later in the evening. I thought they should keep working through the day and only rest at night. Then they wouldn't have to stay up so late. In another country where people rested in the afternoons, office workers also had a six-day work week! I thought that if they did not take afternoon rests, they could easily have a five-day work week. A number of us became upset when our husbands followed the local six-day week and worked 8-hour days rather than 6-hour days. We convinced the leaders to close the office on Saturdays so our husbands could spend more time with their families.

Another misunderstanding I experienced in regard to rest practices was with co-workers from Strong Structure countries. One colleague told us not to call her family during the time they had their meals or when they were resting in the afternoon and evening. I thought it was inappropriate to be so straightforward in telling us what we could and couldn't do, but later I realized she came from a Strong Structure culture that had strict rules about rest activities.

I was also shocked when I learned that in some cultures mothers slept with their children rather than with their husbands. In another country a mother slept on floor mats with her children while the father slept alone on a regular bed. I assumed the father would give his bed to the mother and children or that he and his wife would sleep together.

In Latin America I had difficulty learning to sleep on a hammock because it moved whenever I moved. In another country I had difficulty adjusting to a mattress filled with kapok, a fiber somewhat similar to cotton, but much coarser.

Resting Spaces

Typical spaces for rest in the home are the places where family members nap or sleep, such as beds, couches, floors, or other flat areas. In hot climates some individuals sleep in hammocks to allow the wind to cool the body; in cooler climates individuals sleep close to a fire or source of heat or on mats on a heated floor, as in Korea. Some US Americans rest during the day on a couch or in an easy chair; in other cultures people consider it wrong to sleep in a chair or a couch. In Individuating cultures people have their own places to rest; people in Strong Community cultures prefer places where more than one person can rest at the same time. Chairs, couches, and beds are all shared in Strong Community cultures, but Individuating cultures value individual rest places. In Strong Community cultures children may be allowed to sleep wherever they fall asleep. Babies may also sleep in a cloth sling carried by their mother or caretaker.

In some homes the rest areas are in the front of the house (some Mexican homes), while in others the rest areas are at the back of the house. In Strong Structure cultures the oldest male may have a separate bedroom. In some Asian countries children sleep with their mother or parents; children in the US normally have a separate bedroom from their parents and sometimes separate bedrooms from their siblings. Some US American spouses sleep in different rooms.

In some Asian cultures it is important for the eldest person (parent or grandparent) to sleep in the back part of the house. The bed itself should also be facing north. In Bali, Indonesia, the bed should face the nearby mountain or volcano instead of the sea (Forshee 2007, 93).

In Individuating or consumer cultures a person takes a break from work by going to another location so that they are not reminded of their work. The primary focus is on work, and social relationships and resting are considered non-work activities. Therefore, social interaction and resting should be kept to a minimumin the workplace.

In Strong Community cultures people believe that the quality of life is fostered through social interaction. Therefore, it is not important to separate rest and work. The focus is more on maintaining good, harmonious relationships. The amount of work that gets done is secondary to maintaining good relationships in the workplace. In fact, people in Strong Community cultures believe that individuals who do not maintain good interpersonal relationships actually bring bad consequences to the community as a whole.

RESTING PRACTICES

Sleep is the primary rest activity around the world. Some people need only 6-7 hours of sleep, but others need more. Recent studies conducted in the United States report that most Americans, both adults and children, lack 1-3 hours of sleep per night (Maas 1999). This means that if US Americans lack 1-3 hours of sleep per night, they lack 7-21 hours of sleep per week and 560-1,068 hours a year. The perceived need to work or play may drive a person to get less sleep than their body requires. The lack of sleep has been shown to contribute to major illnesses such as heart disease, cancer, diabetes, and obesity (Stein 2005).

In warmer climates many people have regular rest times during the hottest time of the day—from two to five in the afternoon. Latin America is well known for its afternoon *siesta*, and in some places government offices and businesses shut down during the rest time and open up again in the evening when it gets cooler.

In industrialized cultures, regular breaks from work are included in the normal workday schedule. The lunchtime break is longer, but some people skip lunch in order to leave work earlier. There are also days off work with or without pay, sick days, and vacation days. Other countries allow employees to take time off from work for family needs such as funerals and illness of family members. Different work practices influence rest practices.

In a Weak Structure culture individuals make their own rules regarding rest. Members in the same family may sleep at different times rather than follow a common pattern. A family member might take a rest one afternoon and not the next depending on his or her preference. An individual may also stay up late and not wake up until midday.

In Strong Structure cultures there are strict rules for times of rest that are enforced either orally or in a written form. The rules regarding rest define when rest hours occur and what may or may not happen during an official time of rest. In a Strong Structure and Weak Community culture there are specific times when social interaction (telephone calls, social visits, etc.) with non-family members are not allowed (e.g.

after 9:00 pm at night or before 8:00 am in the morning.) Similarly people would not expect to be disturbed by outside calls or visitors during meal times. Laws about rest may also define the acceptable noise level as well as what constitutes noise (e.g., disturbing the peace).

In Strong Structure cultures, the father or the oldest male may have his own sleeping room, while the mother or grandmother sleeps with the children and/or grandchildren. Tradition determines where family members sleep based on birth order, age, or gender. The oldest male has the most desirable location and best sleeping facilities (bed, sheets, blankets, pillows).

In Weak Community cultures rest activities are individual rather than group events. There is not an agreed upon time for everyone to rest. Each person takes responsibility for when and how long he or she rests. Although a person looks tired, the individual person is responsible to make decisions about his or her own rest. The ideal in Weak Community is also for each individual to have his or her own sleeping place. If they have to share, they would complain about it.

In a Strong Community culture, rest is a communal activity and everyone either rests at the same time or respects the rest time. It is not unusual for Strong Community family members to rest in the same bed and not make distinctions according to age, gender, or birth order. The time of resting is a general, not a fixed time. In parts of Indonesia the family shuts the front door during the afternoon rest. When the front door is open it indicates that the family has finished their rest. In Strong Community cultures people take responsibility for others and freely tell someone to rest during the rest time. Strong Community cultures also share sleeping space, such as beds or floor mats. In a round house people may sleep in a circle with their feet towards the fire.

CBJS and Resting

Your present day rest practices have been influenced by your work practices and cultural values.

If you are from a Weak Structure culture, you may get frustrated, upset, or angry when:

- you aren't able to sleep in your own bed with your own pillow, bedding, and mattress

- you don't have a choice about the rules about when or where to rest

- people are given a better place to rest due to their age, gender, or status

If you are from a Weak Structure culture, you may get frustrated, upset, or angry when:

- complaining about different rest practices for higher and lower status people

- getting angry when you are not able to rest well due to not being able to have your sleep preferences

If you are from a Strong Structure culture, you may get frustrated, upset, or angry when:

- rules for resting are not clear or if you are expected to make your own decisions about when or where to rest

- higher status people are not given better places to rest

- you are given a better rest place than a higher status person

Your belief in Strong Structure justifies:

- punishing people who do not follow the rest rules

- giving particular rest benefits to higher status people

- not allowing lower status people to rest as much as higher status people

If you are from a Weak Community family, you may get frustrated, upset, or angry when:

- others tell you that you look tired or need to rest

- others want to share your bed or sleep in the same room

Your belief in Weak Community justifies:

- telling others that when and how long you sleep is your decision

- not allowing others to share your bed or sleep in the same room

- criticizing rest practices that are different than yours

If you are from a Strong Community culture, you may get frustrated, upset, or angry when:

- people expect you to sleep in a separate bed or room

- people don't follow the group's decision to rest or not rest

- a person challenges the group's decision regarding rest

Your belief in Strong Community justifies:

- punishing the person who doesn't share their bed or room or challenges the group's decision about rest

Your CbJS about resting practices can distort the image of God in your decision making, beliefs, and emotions.

How Resting Practices Distort the Image of God

I had thought that it was proper to work only five days a week and never on Saturday or Sunday. However, God commanded the Israelites to work six days and rest one day (Exodus 20:8-11). I judged the six-day week of working from my own cultural background.

I also thought people who took naps in the afternoon were basically lazy. However, when I couldn't stay awake in the heat of the afternoon sun, I realized the wisdom in taking an afternoon rest.

I didn't realize how my Individuating cultural values influenced my rest practices. I didn't think it was right to not make my own decision in regard to where I slept and when I slept. I thought it was biblical to have a personal choice.

When I think back to my time overseas, I would sleep fitfully and wake up early thinking about all the things I needed to do that day. Consequently I didn't get sufficient rest at night. When I read Psalm 4:8 and Psalm 127:2, I realized that I was trying to do too many things and I was not committing my activities to God and resting in the wisdom He could give me.

God's definition of rest includes spiritual as well as physical rest. I was trying to do so much by my own effort and I wasn't resting in God. In these ways my culture was distorting the image of God.

Exercise

...8A: Childhood Resting Practices

1. Describe where, how many hours, when, and with whom you slept in your childhood home.

2. Do you generally get a good night's rest? What helps or hinders your rest?

3. How do you distinguish your work from other activities you do at home?

4. Explain if you think you should spend more or less time working than you do.

Culture Based Judging System Question #6:

Resting

Choose the statement that best describes your preference regarding rest and sleep. I prefer...

__1. a flexible work/sleep schedule, not the same every day, and I prefer to sleep in my own bed. I don't like rigid schedules.

__2. a set work/sleep schedule that is the same every day and follows clear guidelines. I don't like surprises.

__3. older and/or higher status people have better sleeping arrangements. I am embarrassed if I get a better bed than an older person.

__4. family members sleep in whatever sleep place is closest when they get tired. We don't like to sleep alone.

Reflection #9:

Resting

1. Think about how your childhood work experiences affect your present day rest practices.

2. Read the following verses. How might your knowledge of cultural rest and work types enable you to get the rest you need each day to deal with the challenges you face at work in a godly way?

   Exodus 20:8; Psalm 4:8; Psalm 127:2; Isaiah 40:28-31; Matthew 11:28-30; Galatians 6:9

3. Share what God is saying to you. Pray for one another.

Exercise

...8B: An Exercise of Reflection and Discussion

Either with a discussion partner or on your own, reflect on these topics and how your family approached these issues during your childhood, your family's set of preferences concerning these topics, and what you and your family values today...

1. Sports. Culturally important sports. How sports reflect Community/Structure values.

2. Vacations. Who takes a vacation? How long is a typical vacation? What activities are considered important/necessary on a vacation? Relation of vacation to work.

3. Games. Favorite games in your childhood/family. Favorite games for your co-workers. Games with cultural significance.

Chapter 9

How Childhood Cleaning Practices Shape your CBJS

The definition of clean and dirty varies from family to family and culture to culture. According to Douglas (1966), in order to understand these differences one first needs to understand the definition of "dirt." Things that are dirty need to be cleaned. Weak Community cultures define dirt as a material substance (such as soil) that is unhealthful or unhygienic because it carries germs. Soaps and detergents are used to remove the dirt. Strong Community cultures define dirt spiritually as something that defiles life in an immaterial sense. Washing with water and conducting appropriate rituals can take away this kind of uncleanness.

Of all the common household activities (visiting, eating, working, resting, and cleaning), cleaning practices are most closely associated with a culture's symbolic value of right and wrong. If appropriate cultural cleaning practices are followed, one is considered physically, morally, and spiritually clean; if appropriate cultural cleaning practices are not followed, one remains physically, morally, and spiritually dirty.

In order to help you better understand the differing assumptions about cleaning practices in various cultures, this chapter discusses cleaning spaces, cleaning activities, the CbJS and cleaning, and an example of how cleaning practices distort the image of God. These topics will help you recall cleaning practices in your childhood home to discover how they impact you today.

A Personal Reflection on Cleaning

Differences in the definition of cleanliness have been a major source of stress to me. The front area of my childhood home was considered clean and guests were welcome there, but the back of the house was considered to be the dirty area and guests were not welcome. My family indicated a dirty area by closing the door. When I lived in different countries and guests opened a closed door in my house, I felt they had violated my privacy. I felt justified in getting upset with them because I thought they were rude.

When we were in one foreign country, we learned that they washed dishes with soapy hot water, but did not rinse the dishes. Although I could not taste the soap, I did not think the dishes were actually clean.

One Asian friend thought that people should use different cloths to wash dishes and to clean kitchen counters. She thought I was not clean because I used the same cloth for these two tasks. I was upset that she thought I was not clean because I thought my way was right.

In some countries various offerings are given to spiritually clean a home, a place of business, or a temple. I felt very uncomfortable in these places and thought that the leaves and flowers that were placed on the ground could in no way "clean" a place.

I had the most difficulty with different toilet practices. After having grown up in the US, I had difficulty adjusting to a squat toilet. I was accustomed to having a toilet seat available. When faced with different cleaning practices and different types of toilets, I never felt very clean and did not realize how much that affected my overall sense of well-being.

CLEANING SPACES

The outside and the inside of the house can be divided using the concept of clean and dirty as defined by different cultures. Some cultures consider the inside of the house to be clean and the outside to be dirty/unclean, while others define certain areas inside as either clean or dirty. Cleaning activities in each culture are determined by these distinctions. The categories of clean and dirty are also closely associated with the concepts of sacred and secular and male and female.

The Weak Community cultures (Individuating and Institutionalizing) define dirt in terms of its material or physical characteristics. Strong Community cultures (Hierarching and Interrelating) use the terms clean and dirty in regard to physical things, but also in regard to social relationships and group harmony. A healer or shaman might diagnose that an illness is caused by interpersonal conflicts and address the situation as a spiritual matter, while a Western doctor would look for physical symptoms and treat with medicine. This underlying difference contributes to constant misunderstanding between Weak and Strong Community cultures. The cultural practices look the same, but the underlying reasons are very different.

In the Old Testament (Joshua 20:4) the whole village was defined as sacred/clean and outside the village as secular/dirty. In Strong Community cultures, such as in Japan and Korea, the inside of the house is clean, while the outside of the house is dirty. Therefore, people remove their shoes at the door to keep the inside of the house clean. The areas where family heirlooms, household gods, or ancestor tablets are kept are regarded as sacred, while other areas in the house are secular. The areas where rituals take place are also sacred.

In some Weak Community cultures the front part of the house (the public area) is clean, while the back (the private area) is dirty. Therefore, more attention is given to keeping the front area clean than the back area.

There are also areas inside or outside the house to remove dirt: e.g., the kitchen, where dirty dishes are washed; the laundry area, where dirty clothes are washed; the toilet for elimination; and the bathing area, where dirty bodies are washed. Cultures that are similar in other ways, such as Great Britain and Australia, may have different definitions of clean and dirty. In British homes clothes are washed near the kitchen, close to eating and cooking activities. In Australian homes cooking and eating are considered clean activities that should not take place close to clothes washing, bathing, and elimination activities.

> Each activity removed dirt from an object, and these objects were brought into conjunction and their cleaning undertaken in one space. The scullery served this purpose until the advent of the gas cooker.... the Australian domestic system has reserved the kitchen for those activities solely related to the preparation of food and dishwashing. A separate laundry was provided, and a separate bathroom taken for granted. Hence dishwashing, laundering, and bathing have traditionally been considered as three different types of activity in Australia. It was not the removal of dirt which provided the signification, but the object—crockery, clothes, the body—which was being cleansed. Therefore three separated spaces were provided for the removal of dirt from three sets of objects (Lawrence 1987, 105).

In some cultures male and female spaces are conceptually similar to clean and dirty spaces. The space in the yurt is divided equally into male and female spaces and between clean and dirty. In Middle Eastern cultures the inside of the house is female, while outside the house is male. In Afghanistan there are certain schools, theaters, and buses spaces for women only in keeping with the separation of male and female (Hafizullah 2005, 175).

Weak Community cultures clean what is considered an inanimate house according to their own preferences (Individuating) or according to a certain set of rules (Institutionalizing). Strong Community cultures clean what is considered a living house, the place where spiritual beings live. They clean the house to maintain the wellbeing of the spirits of the living and the dead. Hierarching cultures clean according to the Hierarchy, while Interrelating cultures clean together in order to maintain harmony between people and the universe. Strong Community cultures also use rituals such as daily or regular cleaning of the four corners of the house, putting out daily offerings, etc. to protect the house from evil influences. They are very aware of the spirit world and its activity in contrast to people in Weak Community.

In the Individuating American home (Figure 9), cleaning spaces are distinguished by function. Dishes are cleaned in the kitchen, clothes in the laundry room, and bodies in the bathroom/toilet. In the Hierarching Asian home (Figure 10), cleaning spaces are in the back outside area—dishes, clothes, and bodies are washed, and eliminating takes place in the back cleaning area next to the source of water. In the Central Asian yurt (Figure 11), cleaning takes places outside the yurt—washing dishes, washing clothes, bathing, and eliminating.

Cleaning Activities

There are two different definitions of cleaning. One is a material/physical definition associated with hygiene; the other is a spiritual definition associated with enhancing the life of the community.

> Body cleansing, like all universal and habitual activities, is subject to ritual uses and to a variety of philosophical and psychological meanings. Ritual cleansing is a practice that can be found in some form among all peoples and in almost all periods of history and still survives in many of the world's religions. Thus, circumcision, the washing of the hands at communion, washing of the feet, bathing in the holy Ganges, and other practices are all body-hygiene practices that have more symbolic than hygienic value. Most commonly purifying rituals such as these are performed after coming into contact with ritually contaminating things, persons, or acts; or before coming into contact with that which is holy—whether this be a person, place, or act to be performed...Contaminants can range from death to menstruation, childbirth, murder, persons of inferior caste, and so on... (Kira 1975, 11).

In the Hindu worldview there are two states of being—pure and impure. A person who is pure is always in danger of being polluted. Contact with natural human waste (such as saliva, urine, feces, semen, or menstrual blood) makes a person impure. When a person dies, the whole family is considered impure, as are the people who handle the body. This impure state lasts for several days until all funeral rites are completed. During this time the family has various things they can and cannot do to keep themselves clean and to keep from getting dirty (Burnett 1988, 80).

Cleaning activities remove dirt. Every aspect of life in the house involves cleaning. Dusting, sweeping, and mopping remove dirt from the house. Washing dishes removes uneaten food, and washing clothes removes dirt. Bathing removes dirt from bodies, and using the toilet eliminates body waste. In the following sections the activities of cleaning (house, dishes, clothes), bathing, and toilet use will be briefly discussed.

Cleaning

The definition of dirt determines how the house is cleaned, how dishes are washed, and how clothes are washed to remove the dirt.

In some Asian houses the floor is considered clean. Therefore, shoes are removed before stepping into the house because shoes are considered dirty. People also eat and sleep on the floor, so there is a greater need to keep the floors clean. In cultures where the floor is considered dirty, such frequent cleaning is not considered necessary.

In some houses, floors are cleaned daily, while other areas in the house are cleaned less frequently. Some cleaning activities, such as dusting and sweeping, may be done daily, while mopping may be done weekly. In some cultures floors are considered clean if they have been washed with water; in other cultures floors are considered clean only if they have been washed with a chemical cleaner. Windows may be washed less frequently.

The definition of dirt determines the frequency of dish washing, how they are washed, and where dishes are washed. Some people clean dishes immediately after eating, while others may leave them for later, even the next day. To clean food off dishes, some cultures use detergent, soap, or ashes. Some groups use cold water, while others prefer to use hot water. Some people wash dishes with a cloth or a brush, while others use only their hands. Some cultures rinse off the soap from the dishes; others do not. Some dry the dishes with a towel; others allow the dishes to dry inside or outside in the sun.

The definition of dirt also determines the frequency of washing clothes, how one washes clothes, and where one washes clothes. Some people wash clothes every day, while others wash once a week or less often. People who live in warm climates tend to wash clothes more frequently than those who live in cooler climates. The frequency of washing bed sheets may also depend on when people bathe. People who bathe in the morning tend to wash their bed sheets more frequently than those who bathe in the evening. Some people wash clothes in machines; others wash clothes by hand using soap or various cleaning aids, such as brushes or rocks to loosen the dirt.

Weak Structure cultures do not have well-established rules for cleaning the house, washing dishes, or washing clothes. They may clean one way this week and another way the next week. There is no regular cleaning schedule. People in Weak Structure groups do not have a problem washing tennis shoes and clothes at the same time. Dishes may be washed after meals or left for the following days. The order of washing is not set. Glasses may be washed before or after utensils. Dishes may be wiped dry, left to dry, or put in the dishwasher to be steam dried.

Strong Structure cultures have strict rules for cleaning the house, washing dishes, and washing clothes. There is a clear order in which items have to be washed or cleaned. There are also rules in regard to what items cannot be washed together (such as tennis shoes and clothes for the Japanese). People in these cultures follow a regular cleaning schedule. Strong Structure cultures might wash glasses first, then plates, and finally eating utensils. The person who is responsible for cleaning makes sure that cleaning is done according to the rules. Separate cloths are used for cleaning different things— dishes, table, counters, and floors. Each cleaning activity is done according to a regular schedule. In a Strong Structure culture, the youngest person may be expected to wash dishes after a certain age.

People in Weak Community cultures prefer to work alone and do not clean the house or wash dishes or clothes with others. They can choose the time that they clean, the frequency they clean, and the manner they clean. The individual takes responsibility to clean or not to clean.

People in Strong Community cultures clean the house, wash dishes, and wash clothes with others. They do not like doing these activities alone. Some Strong Community cultures have a communal washing area where women gather to clean and wash and socialize at the same time. People in Strong Community cultures also take responsibility for getting others to help with cleaning activities.

Bathing

The definition of dirt also determines the time of bathing, how one bathes, and where one bathes. Some prefer bathing in the evening to remove the day's dirt; others prefer bathing in the morning to be clean before they go to work. People who live in hot climates may bathe more than once a day; those who live in cooler climates may bathe less frequently. The manner of bathing is also influenced by the availability of water. Some people bathe in a tub of water; others under a flow of water; while others pour a dipper over themselves after they have scrubbed with soap, as in Indonesia (Forshee 2006, 87). People in some cultures use cold water to bathe; others use hot water. Many cultures have private baths, but the Japanese and Russians (among others) have public baths. In public baths people scrub themselves clean prior to entering the bath.

In contrast to baths that use only water, the Finnish use hot steam. A person sits in a room (sauna) with hot steam for a period of time until the body sweats, cleaning out the impurities and loosening the dead skin. These baths are also used for medicinal purposes to relax the muscles after a hard day's work. Other sweat baths are the Roman *balneae* and *thermae*, the Turkish *hammam*, the Native American sweat lodge, and the *temascal* in Mexico and Guatemala.

Body odor is also related to the concept of cleanliness. Familiar smells are considered clean and unfamiliar smells are dirty. Different kinds of foods produce different kinds of body odors. Diets of meat and dairy products produce body odors that are considered offensive by people who rarely eat meat and dairy products. People who eat primarily tubers and vegetables have a distinctive body odor. An unfamiliar body odor is considered dirty.

Some cultures (e.g., Korean) have a special word for dead skin or body dirt, and they use a special brush or rough cloth to scrub off the dead skin. English-speaking Americans do not have a word for dead skin and do not normally focus on scrubbing off the dead skin in their bathing. Some Asians consider the odor of dead skin to be dirty and offensive. On the other hand US Americans are offended by the body odor caused by eating garlic, fish, tubers, etc. They prefer the smell of commercial perfumes and deodorants to these body odors.

Weak Structure cultures do not usually have a set of rules for bathing. There is no set order in which family members bathe and no set time for bathing or cleaning. The individual decides when to clean and when to bathe. No one takes responsibility for the cleanliness of others, but only for themselves and their individual family.

Strong Structure cultures have a definite order for bathing that specifies the oldest or highest status person to take the first bath. Others have to wait their turn. Bathing activities in Strong Structure may follow the order of oldest male or the highest status person first down to the youngest or lowest status person last. The oldest person gets the hottest water and better cleaning materials.

In Weak Community cultures individuals expect to clean and wash individually. They do not consider that their cleaning may conflict with others who may want to clean at the same time. Weak Community values individual bathing resources and individual bathing. People in Weak Community cultures don't expect to share cleaning activities or cleaning materials (e.g., bath water).

Strong Community cleaning activities tend to be carried out by the family or the community rather than individually. There is community use of bathing resources—either bathing together and/or using the same bath water. In the Strong Community Native American sweat lodges the body and the mind are considered to be brought into accord with supernatural powers. It is not the sweat that cleans and cures, but the power of the spirits. Public baths are also common in Strong Community cultures.

Toilet Use

Toilets vary from culture to culture in terms of the location, the visibility, and the type of waste system. Some cultures have toilet facilities outside the house; others have them inside the house. Some cultures have the toilet in the same room as bathing facilities (as in the US), while others have separate rooms for the toilet and bathing (as in Australia). When able, US Americans add more bathrooms to their house to promote individual use. They also treat the bathroom as a place to be decorated, while others, such as Indonesians, consider the bathroom and toilet as places to get rid of bodily dirt/waste and not something to decorate (Forshee 2006, 87).

Cultures also differ in the visibility of toilet facilities. People in some cultures consider toilet use a very private affair and take offense if public toilets are not completely enclosed. Other cultures are comfortable with less enclosed structures. In some cultures, privacy is created by people turning their head or looking the other way to give others privacy rather than by an enclosed physical structure.

Outdoor facilities use the earth system of waste disposal—either burying the waste or allowing it to decompose. Some places use waste materials for fertilizer for plants or fuel for fires.

In addition to the natural environment, there are two other main kinds of toilets around the world—flush and squat toilets. Flush toilets use more water to flush away waste material. There are different kinds of flush toilets. Some toilets have two flush options—a smaller one for urine and a larger one for feces. There are also different shapes of toilet bowls. Some toilets have larger toilet bowls so that the feces can be examined for worms before flushing. US Americans find this unhygienic and do not like to look at their body waste. They leave this for lab examiners (Bray 2004). The Japanese have developed computerized functions for the toilet (e.g., temperature, deodorizing, flushing).

The US American sense of privacy requires a lock on the bathroom (toilet) door on the inside to prevent others from entering. In other cultures there are no locks on the bathroom doors or in some cases not even doors, but only pieces of cloth or curtains. Others do not use a door covering.

Squat toilets are found in many parts of the world, but not in the United States and Europe. Squat toilets conserve on water and have no mechanical parts. People who use squat toilets do not use toilet paper. Instead they use water that is either in buckets or piped in. The flushing mechanism is not as strong as a flush toilet, and the smell of urine and human waste often remains. The floors of squat toilets are normally wet. Instead of toilet paper some people use water (Russia, Japan, Korea, Malaysia, Thailand, Italy), rope (China, Iran), pebbles (Egypt), stones (Mongolia) and leaves (Kenya) (Bray 2004).

Cummings (2000) suggests that anthropologists describing other cultures have overlooked the toilet as a window to cross-cultural understanding. His training did not prepare him for his cross-cultural frustrations with squat toilets and dip baths. For individuals who use squat toilets, learning to use the seat on flush toilets can be just as frustrating. Sitting on the seat of flush toilets can be as difficult as learning to use a squat toilet.

In some cultures dirt is believed to transmit germs and bacteria. In these cultures, the best way to get rid of the dirt is through bathing and toilet use, and it is important for people to be completely separated from dirt as quickly as possible, particularly toilet dirt.

> Urine and feces, in particular, are generally regarded by contemporary Western society as filth of the worst sort, so much so that the individual not only wants to dispose of them as thoroughly and quickly as possible but also wishes in many instances to be completely disassociated from the act of producing them (Kira 1975, 93).

The smell of urine and feces is offensive to those who view cleanliness as hygienic. These cultures have many kinds of cleaners and deodorizers to get rid of the odor. For others the smell of urine and feces is not offensive, but merely a part of human life. In such cultures there is no need to use cleaners or deodorizers. Cow urine is used as a cleaning agent in Hindu cultures.

Cultural practices associated with the toilet provide a window on the particular culture. Normally hand washing also accompanies the use of the toilet. Kira (1975, 11) reports that in France, men wash their hands before using the toilet, while British men wash their hands afterwards. Whatever practices are followed become the right way of cleaning and washing, while other ways become the wrong way.

In Weak Structure cultures toilet use is individual and normally a Weak Structure person does not like waiting to use the toilet.

In Strong Structure cultures toilet use is determined by age or status. Younger people or lower status people are trained to wait for older or higher status people to use the toilet first.

In Weak Community cultures toilet use is individual and this person prefers to use the toilet facilities alone.

In Strong Community cultures toilet use is communal and this person doesn't mind sharing facilities with others. These cultures might also have toilet and bathing facilities close to each other as water keeps both clean.

CBJS and Cleaning

In English language Western cultures people say, "cleanliness is close to godliness." You may be surprised to discover the ways in which your definition of "clean" and "dirty" affects your responses to cultural differences.

If you are from a Weak Structure culture, you may get frustrated, upset, or angry when:

- you have to take your shoes off before going inside the house
- you have to follow different cleaning rules
- the cleaning activities are different from yours
- only lower status people clean
- you are the youngest person and are expected to wash dishes
- children are not allowed to use the toilet before older people

Your belief in Weak Structure justifies:

- ignoring rules about taking your shoes off inside the house
- re-cleaning things were not cleaned according to your rules
- criticizing different cleaning practices
- complaining about the different treatment for people with higher status

- telling other people besides the youngest person to wash dishes

If you are from a Strong Structure culture, you may get frustrated, upset, or angry when:

- the rules are not followed in regard to cleaning (shoes and clothes are washed together, shoes are worn inside)

- older or higher status people are not expected to bathe first or in better facilities

- children are allowed to use the cleaning facilities before older or higher status people

- someone doesn't accept your help with cleaning activities

- you follow the rules even if you don't like them

Your belief in Strong Structure justifies:

- speaking to or punishing people who don't clean according to the rules

- criticizing people who don't treat older and higher status people better

- scolding or punishing lower status people (children) who use cleaning facilities before older or higher status people

If you are from a Weak Community family, you may get frustrated, upset, or angry when:

- others want to help you clean your house, dishes, clothes

- others tell you to take a bath

- people expect you to bathe with the group

Your belief in Weak Community justifies:

- telling people that you do your cleaning by yourself

- criticizing different cleaning activities (e.g., group bathing)

- causing people to lose face by telling them their cleaning practices aren't really clean

Strong Community individuals get frustrated, upset, or angry when:

- cleaning activities were not done together and bathing materials were not shared
- people do not take group suggestions to clean, wash, or bathe
- you conform but harbor bad feelings about it

Your belief in Strong Community justifies:

- helping people clean even if they have refused your help
- gossiping about those who don't keep to the group's standard of cleanliness

Your CbJS about cleaning practices can distort the image of God in your decision making, beliefs, and emotions.

How Cleaning Practices Distort the Image of God

I think the definition of clean and dirty is probably the most shocking or difficult to deal with of all the topics you have considered in the previous chapters. I judged other cultural practices based on my own definition of clean and dirty. I considered people to be dirty because they did not rinse the soap off their dishes. However, there is no Scripture that condemns that practice. I looked down on the Asians who insisted on using different cleaning cloths for dishes and counters, but there was no Scripture that condemns that. There is no Scripture that says "keep out if there is a closed door," and there is no Scripture that says chemical detergents are better than water for cleaning floor or toilets. I preferred flush toilets to squat toilets because that was how I was raised. I was more comfortable with my cultural beliefs and therefore I judged others by my cultural standards.

When I looked into Scripture (see below), I realized that cleanliness was associated with God's character of holiness and being made clean from a guilty conscience. It is God's Word that makes me clean and not particular cultural practices. God wants me to be more concerned about being clean on the inside than the outside. I was allowing different cultural practices of outward cleanliness to determine what I considered was right or wrong rather than God's standard of inward cleanliness. My definition of right and wrong prevented me from accepting others and distorted God's image in me.

∽

Exercise

...9A: Childhood Cleaning Practices

1. Describe how frequently you clean your house, wash dishes, wash clothes, and bathe.

2. How was dish washing and clothes washing done in your childhood home.

3. What kind of bathing and toilet (elimination) practices did you have in your childhood home (what kind of cleaners did you use, when did you bathe/use the toilet, what did the bath/toilet look like, where was it, frequency of cleaning, etc.)

∽

Culture Based Judging System Question #8:

Cleaning

Choose the statement that best describes the cleaning practices in your childhood home.[34]

__1. My parents let me clean my room the way I wanted. I would get upset if someone told me how to clean my room.

__2. I was expected to follow directions to keep my room clean. I don't like it if there are not clear directions for cleaning.

__3. The cleaning chores were assigned by status. I would get upset if I someone from the wrong status cleaning the house.

__4. The cleaning chores were divided equally among all family members. I would get upset if a family member did not want to clean with the family members.

～

REFLECTION #10:

CLEANING

1. Think about how your co-workers' different ways of cleaning reflect one of the four cultural types. In what way does your way of cleaning reflect your childhood cleaning practices?

2. Read these verses about God's standard of cleanliness and how you should respond to your co-workers' different cleaning practices (both physical and spiritual):

   Matthew 15:10-11, 18-20; 23:25; Mark 7:20-22; Luke 11:38-42; Hebrews 10:22; John 15:3

3. Share with someone what God is telling you and pray for one another.

～

EXERCISE

...9B: An Exercise of Reflection and Discussion

Either with a discussion partner or on your own, reflect on these topics and how your family approached these issues during your childhood, your family's set of preferences concerning these topics, and what you and your family values today...

1. Formal/informal spiritual activities. What is considered "spiritual" and what is "not spiritual"?

2. Religious specialists- what are they allowed to do and perform? Expectations of non-specialists in religious activities.

3. Religious beliefs and practices concerning what is clean.

4. Ritual cleaning activities. Daily/monthly/annual cycles.

5. Illnesses. Categories/causes of illness. Ideal treatment of illness. Maintaining health.

6. Aging. Physical impairment. Deformity. How older people are treated.

Chapter 10

HOW TO APPLY BIBLICAL
TRUTH TO YOUR CBJS

The main purpose of this book is to foster biblical multicultural teams by helping you apply biblical truth to cultural differences. The book has introduced a series of topics. We started by explaining what it means to be made in the image of God. Second, we explored how the CbJS of our cultural type replaces biblical truth and distorts the image of God. Finally, we looked at ways to apply biblical truth to cultural differences in order to foster biblical multicultural teams: teams where individual team members from different cultures are thriving and flourishing by clearly reflecting the image of God.

In Chapter 1 we discussed what it means to be made in the image of God through our decision making, beliefs, and emotions. Although we have been created in God's image, as a result of our human nature we have developed cultural ways of doing things that do not align with God's way. Therefore, when we encounter cultural differences, our CbJS (Chapter 2) kicks in to maintain our cultural type. We make decisions based on our preferred type of decision making (individual, system, group consensus) based on human knowledge or beliefs and our emotions (heart) respond negatively (frustration, upset, anger) to cultural differences. Because we have been doing things in the same way for so many years, we automatically believe our way is the right and biblical way. We are unable to explain our negative responses to cultural differences.

Chapters 3-9 applied these principles to your childhood experience. You traced how your CbJS was shaped by your childhood family interaction (nurture and discipline, Chapter 3) and by the structure of your childhood home (Chapter 4). By sharing about your home with others you should have gained a better understanding of why you like or dislike certain things about your present physical or social environment. You may also have discovered how many cultural values are reflected in the use of space and the activities in each room. In chapters 5-9 you went through each room of your childhood home reflecting on visiting (Chapter 5), eating (Chapter 6), working (Chapter 7), resting (Chapter 8), and cleaning (Chapter 9) practices. The readings, questions, and reflections in each chapter were intended to help you realize how your CbJS shaped your cultural preferences in present day situations.

Although you have gone through the material in the book, it may still be difficult for you to understand how to address cultural differences with biblical truth. Therefore, in this final chapter we will expand on the main points—what it means to be made in the image of God, how our CbJS distorts the image of God, and how to apply biblical truth to cultural differences.

What it Means to be Made in the Image of God

Being made in the image of God is the most basic point in the book. If you do not believe you are made in the image of God, it will be difficult for you to accept others as also made in the image of God. You will also have difficulty fostering biblical multicultural teams. Being created in God's image means having the ability to make godly decisions based on God's truths that affect your emotions towards yourself and others.

One proof that you believe you are created in God's image is a willingness and openness to develop relationships with people from other cultures, who are also part of God's image. If you find yourself avoiding interaction with people from other cultures, or complaining and criticizing the way they do things, or finding a strong attraction only to those from your own culture, your understanding of what it means to be created in the image of God is not yet aligned with Scripture. Being limited by your cultural perspective is not what God intended when He created humans in His image. Therefore, the first issue you need to address is your understanding of what it means to be created in God's image.

Being created in the image of God means that we were created to be like God. Just as God makes decisions, we have the ability to make decisions. Just as God represents truth, we have the ability to think and apply Truth, and just as God produces a community that loves others, we have the ability to develop loving relationships. However, because we are also affected by the Fall, our decision making, thinking and emotions do not always reflect God's perfection. When our decision making is only based on cultural truth and guided by your cultural desires, you do not reflect God's image. Instead you are characterized by ungodly emotions and behaviors—avoidance, complaints, pride, criticism, frustration, jealousy, bitterness, anger, etc. You begin to keep lists of the wrongs others have committed toward you, you think of how to punish or pay back these wrongs, and become very unpleasant. Some of these negative responses stem from how you were treated in your childhood home. These issues are often unconscious and deep seated. Although this material can be of some help in such cases, counseling is also recommended for deep-seated and long-standing problems.

Once you begin to understand what it means to be made in God's image, you also begin to realize what your life should look like—part of a community united in Christ that is reconciling with each other, loving one another, serving one another, and helping each other to develop their particular God-given spiritual gifts. If these actions do not characterize the interactions of your multicultural team, then it is most likely that the team members are acting in line with their cultural identities rather than following their biblical identities as members of the Body of Christ.

When team members understand what it means to be made in the image of God, then their decision making will choose to depend on God's wisdom based on God's Word and will demonstrate the fruit of the Spirit, reconciliation, unity, and peace. Team members will also understand how their CbJS distorts the image of God and will seek to restore God's image in their own life and in the life of the team.

How your CBJS Distorts the Image of God

In order to recognize how your CbJS distorts the image of God, you first needed to identify your cultural type. It may not have been easy to identify your cultural type if you function in more than one cultural environment. It is also possible to be a combination of types. Aspects of different cultures can look like each of the other types, but there is usually a preference for either Strong or Weak Structure and Strong or Weak Community. If you do not think you have a preference for only one of the four types (Individuating, Institutionalizing, Hierarching, or Interrelating), you can still identify your tendency towards Strong or Weak Structure and Strong or Weak Community. Another way to discover your cultural type is to ask a friend from another culture to identify your type based on his or her observation of your cultural preferences. Individuating and Institutionalizing people find it hardest to identify their cultural type because people in these types get their identity from being an individual and not from belonging to a group.

The review of your family may have reminded you of happy childhood experiences or it may have reminded you of sad, disappointing, or angry experiences. You discovered how your parents showed preferences based on birth order, gender, or other characteristics, and realized how that influences your view of who you are today. You learned how the way you were nurtured and disciplined has shaped your present day decision making of right and wrong. During your reflection you saw how your childhood interaction with your parents resembles your present-day interactions with authority figures or how sibling rivalries relate to your difficulties with co-workers. These activities were included to help you also learn how your childhood family interactions have shaped your CbJS; that is, your decision making based on cultural truths that produces negative emotions towards cultural differences.

The cultural judging questions and exercises at the end of each chapter were designed to help you discover how your CbJS replaces biblical truths. I trust you realized that the key to identifying your CbJS was your negative emotional responses to cultural differences. These emotions (shock, avoidance, frustration, feeling upset, anger, pride, etc.) reveal that you were following cultural truth rather than God's truth. If your emotional responses to cultural differences were love, joy, peace, etc., those positive emotions would validate your belief in God's truth. However, our typical multicultural interactions do not demonstrate the fruit of the Spirit. Instead they demonstrate a distortion of the image of God—stress, complaining, frustration, unhappiness, anger, jealousy, envy, bitterness, pride, etc. Our emotions reveal the state of our hearts and the state of our hearts comes from our decision making based on human beliefs.

As Christians, the main difficulty with our CbJS is that we mistake our cultural values and preferences (our truth) for biblical truth. Because we have been doing things in a particular way for a long period of time we view our way as the right way, the biblical way. We believe that the patterns and preferences that have worked for us should work for others. Therefore, when we encounter cultural differences, we judge the differences to be wrong (unbiblical). We justify or rationalize our negative reactions to others because we have judged their actions to be unbiblical.

When we view our own cultural ways as right and biblical, we also believe our organizational structures are biblical. We have difficulty believing that the policies and structure of our particular organization (e.g., mission, school) do not foster the image of God. However, what we say and do are two different things. As Christians we say we believe others are made in God's image, but we do not always treat them as made in God's image. We do not put personnel, time, or finances into helping people from other cultures feel like they are respected for who they are. Most global organizations now have multicultural memberships, but it is inevitable that there will be structures and policies that make it difficult for people from different cultural backgrounds to flourish and thrive within the cultural base of the original structures (e.g. non-Westerners in American structure).

Two members of the diversity committee of an evangelical university in the United States say that a university that desires to adequately address diversity (multiculturalism) requires: 1) a sound theological basis (e.g., being created in the image of God); 2) that the theological basis is embedded in the university vision, mission statement, and overall plan; 3) that the CEO is on board and models humility and openness; 4) that the university strategy seeks to transform systems and structures in order to effectively nurture a community committed to biblical justice, diversity, and the dignity of all believers; and 5) that the CEO and leadership recognize that authority and power are a stewardship that is to be leveraged for the benefit of all those they lead.[35]

Leaders who are acting biblically are able to identify the false beliefs that lead to their negative emotional responses and are willing to change their beliefs in order to align with biblical truth. They deeply desire to help others examine their false beliefs and align them with biblical truth. They use their positions of authority to ensure that those under them are treated justly and are made to feel they belong. They are willing to ask forgiveness for community sins even though they themselves were not personally involved. They do this to continue the reconciliation process that Christ initiated by reconciling them. They set an example for others to do the same. They are also willing to examine organizational structures and policies to remove things that hinder people from thriving in the multicultural context and are willing to make necessary changes. They provide cultural self-awareness training for all levels in the organization and work to establish an infrastructure to continue improving multicultural sensitivity.

The majority of large mission organizations established in the past 150 years have US American roots. A number of American values are unconsciously embedded in these organizational structures. Most of the financial policies are based on requirements of the state in which the organization was originally registered. Each field office has the autonomy and responsibility to make rules or policies specific to their location. Rules about personnel issues are typically written in order to help administrators make decisions which align with the organizations' values and government regulations. These organizations also set up an orderly procedure to oversee work by establishing a reporting relationship between supervisors and people at lower levels; e.g., a form that both the supervisor and supervisee go over each year to review past work and plan future actions. Many of these mission organizations are based on individuals finding their personal support (i.e. "faith" missions). In these groups each member takes care of his or her own needs, and funds are not usually pooled.

In Strong Community cultures resources and finances are shared. Interpersonal problems are dealt with case by case rather than by policy as each person may have a different set of circumstances that contributes to the problem they are facing. The community is expected to share in the responsibility for interpersonal problems rather than the individuals themselves. Written reports are not required, because people know what others are doing in Strong Community.

Strong Structure organizations have a clear line of authority with an orderly structure for different positions. People who are from the same culture as the organization know their place in the structure and can function accordingly. However, when people from other Strong Structure cultures join the organization, their understanding of the standards may not be the same and, as a result, there can be much confusion.

Many US American organizations have a structure that changes frequently due to Individuating people in it. This is very frustrating for non Americans who are trying to learn the system. Furthermore, when people from different Strong Structure cultures join an organization, they need to find out where they fit in according to their status. When they discover that their status doesn't fit the new structure, they can feel out of place and frustrated. They will need to figure out how to find their place. They may try to do this by doing what is acceptable in their culture, e.g., knocking others down or preventing others from gaining status. Low Structure cultures are generally unaware of status differentiation and often play into the status game by helping lower status people gain higher status. However, people from Strong Structure cultures have difficulty accepting status that is achieved in a culturally different way. There is a great need for Weak and Strong Structure cultures to recognize how their CbJSs may enable others to distort the image of God.

Examples of cultural truths that distort the image of God are:

- Weak Structure fosters the belief "we are better than others" or that "we are not as good as others" or "we don't belong." These beliefs justify competing with others to look better or making others look bad in order to feel better. It also justifies individual pride and self pity.

- Strong Structure fosters the belief that "we are not all equal" and that "some are better than others." These beliefs justify treating higher status people better and treating lower status people worse. It also justifies knocking oth ers down or preventing others from gaining status in order to find one's place.

- Weak Community fosters the belief that "I can succeed in life by myself" and "I don't need others." These beliefs justify a focus on the individual rather than on others. It also justifies hoarding resources rather than sharing with others.

- Strong Community fosters the belief that "our group is not a part of other groups" or that "we can succeed in life without the resources from other groups." These beliefs justify excluding other groups from group activities and resources.

Although Scriptures tell us that these beliefs are false, we find it difficult to let go of these beliefs because our repeated actions over the years have reinforced these beliefs. We need to break our bondage to these false beliefs and the emotional comfort they have given us because they distort God's image in us and prevent us from being the people God created us to be as made in His image.

The false belief of Weak Structure that we are better than others needs to be replaced with God's truth in Philippians 2:3-4: we are to consider others better than ourselves rather than to think of ourselves as better than others. The belief that we are not as good as others needs to be replaced with God's truth expressed in 1 John 4:7 that says everyone who loves has been born of God and knows God.

The false belief of Strong Structure that we are not all equal or some are better than others needs to be replaced with the teaching of James 2:1 that we are not to show favoritism. The belief that we can knock down others or prevent them from succeeding needs to be replaced by Jesus' teaching recorded in Matthew 7:12—we are commanded to treat others as we would like to be treated.

The false belief of Weak Community that we can succeed by ourselves needs to be replaced with the truth about the body of Christ outlined in 1 Corinthians 12:21 that explains we can't say we don't need others and 1 Corinthians 12:16 where it says we can't say we don't belong.

The false belief of Strong Community that our group is better than others and therefore we exclude others from our interactions and resources needs to be replaced by the truth found in Galatians 3:28 that there is neither Jew nor Greek, slave nor free, male or female, as we are all one in Christ.

In Figure 12 the four cultural types are depicted as a whole, but are also separated by two intersecting lines that form a cross. Sherwood Lingenfelter,[36] who has studied and taught anthropology within the Christian context, has stated that applying biblical truths to cultural differences requires going through the cross.

Our emotions signal our beliefs, whether they are false or true. If we desire to change our false beliefs, we need to return to the source, our maker, and ask God for His wisdom. Therefore, it is necessary to spend time studying God's Word and talking to God about how to apply biblical truths to cultural differences.

Figure 12: Going Through the Cross

Structure and Community Theory

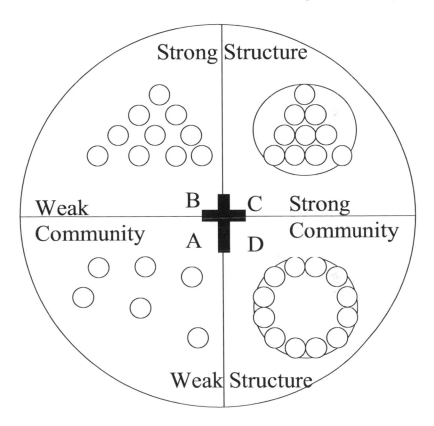

How to Apply Biblical Truth to Cultural Differences

Once you have begun to understand what it means to be made in the image of God and have identified how the CbJS of your cultural type distorts the image of God, then you can begin to seek God's wisdom in how to apply biblical truth to cultural differences.

Although I am frequently asked how each type in and of itself can reflect God's image, the more appropriate question is "How do the four types reflect God's image?" The answer is "together." That is, if we are all created in God's image to be part of the body of Christ, the members of the body of Christ cannot operate on their own, but need the other parts to be whole. In order to understand how this works, we will review Douglas's model of culture once again.

Douglas views the four types as part of a whole in which the strengths of one type are the weaknesses of the other types. In other words, one type exists because of the weaknesses of another type. The Individuating culture exists because of the lack of attention to the individual in Institutionalizing, Hierarching and Interrelating cultures. That is, the rigid rules of the Institutionalizing type, the strict social status of the Hierarching type, and the group consensus process of the Interrelating type take away Individuating choice and responsibility.

Institutionalizing exists because of the excesses of the Individuating focus on personal choice, the tradition and group pressure of the Hierarching type, and the Interrelating group pressure for decision making based on equality.

Hierarching exists due to the excesses of the self focus of Individuating and Institutionalizing types and the lack of concern for orderly structure in the Individuating and Interrelating types.

Interrelating exists due to the focus on the individual in the Individuating type and the focus on an orderly structure that automatically creates inequality in the Institutionalizing and Hierarching types.

The strength of Individuating is that the individual can choose to rely on God to make decisions and does not have to rely on human rules (Institutionalizing), tradition (Hierarching), or group consensus (Interrelating). However, the weakness of Individuating is that they generally do not take others into account and need Hierarching and Interrelating to make them aware of how their individual decisions impact others. They can also learn how to be more orderly from Institutionalizing and Hierarching types.

The strength of Institutionalizing people is creating an orderly society and learning to be obedient by following the rules. If they diligently follow God's rules, Institutionalizing people can more easily reflect the image of God. However, Institutionalizing people are not good about questioning whether the rules are right or wrong or recognizing abuse of authority. They need Individuating people to help them question the rules and to recognize abuses of authority. They also are not aware of others and need Hierarching and Interrelating types to raise their awareness of others.

The strength of Hierarching is loyalty to the group, respect for those in authority, and care for one another in an orderly manner. However, the weakness of Hierarching people is the potential abuse of authority by the leaders, the potential abuse by the community to put social pressure on others to conform, and the exclusion of others who are not in their group. They need Individuating and Interrelating people to critique them.

The strength of Interrelating people is the equal sharing of resources and taking care of one another. The weakness of Interrelating people is the use of social pressure to make decisions that are not based on biblical principles. They need Individuating and Institutionalizing people to recognize the use of social pressure.

If people from Individuating, Institutionalizing, Hierarching, and Interrelating cultures are working together on a regular basis and are open and honest about their weaknesses, they will invite the interaction from the other types to help them reflect God's image more clearly together.

Furthermore, because the particular false beliefs of the cultural types (Weak and Strong Structure and Weak and Strong Community) are developed over a long period of time, it takes time to identify and address them. Two effective methods to help identify and address these problems are studying Scripture and reflective prayer.

Studying Scripture

Spending time in Scripture is important to maintaining our relationship with God. Several Scripture passages have been helpful to me in understanding how my CbJS distorts the image of God.

The first is Romans 1:18-31, that talks about God's wrath against sin. In verse 19-20 it says that God has made Himself known to everyone so no one has a valid excuse to not worship God and follow God's ways. The following verses talk about the cycle of sin that takes us away from God (verses 21-31). Verse 21 explains that the cycle of sin begins when we do not thank God or give God glory. Instead of worshipping the glory of the true God, we worship images of created beings, be they humans or animals, and exchange God's truth for lies by worshipping the created things rather than the Creator. We end up full of every kind of sin and we approve of people who sin.

As I considered these verses I realized that my life did not demonstrate God's truth. Instead of thanking God and giving Him the glory for everything in my life, I complained about others, and was stressed out over numerous situations, frustrated, upset, and even angry. Instead of worshipping God, I was worshipping my cultural ideal, myself. This led to believing lies about myself rather than believing God's truth. If I believed that God is Lord of all and worthy of my praise and thanksgiving, I needed to develop the daily practice of thanking Him and giving Him glory. I had many reasons to thank God. When I began to do this, God began to fill my life with peace, joy, and love for others. Slowly God revealed to me the lies that had darkened my heart and He began help me replace them with His truth.

When my CbJS was at work, it revealed a lot about my preferences and values. The things for which I judged others were actually true of my own life (Romans 2:1-4). In judging others I was bringing God's judgment on myself, and at the same time showing contempt for God's kindness, tolerance, and patience that should have led me to repentance.

Another biblical truth that helped me grasp more of the image of God is the truth explained in Revelation 5:7 and 7:9, which depict Heaven full of people from every tribe, people, language, and nation united in praise and worship before God's throne. I used to think that being Japanese American was not as good as being a European American. However, when I read these verses, I realized that God's image somehow reflects race and ethnicity and that our ethnicity will be evident in Heaven. God also helped me understand that no single culture can understand God fully, and that I need to learn more about Him from other cultural perspectives. In struggling through cultural issues, I have an opportunity to learn more about who God is as well as who I am.

The Scripture verses at the end of chapters 2-11 have also helped me understand and apply biblical truth in my cross-cultural ministry. I encourage you to read and study these biblical truths to see what God wants you to learn.

Reflective Prayer

Many of us live such busy lives we often don't take enough time to talk to God. If we believe that God created us and knows everything about us, we would be spending more time in prayer, giving Him praise and thanks, talking to Him, and asking His advice.

Reflection #2 in chapter 2 can help you to help you reflect on various cultural conflicts you have experienced. I encourage you to reflect on each conflict to see whether you chose to depend on God, whether your thinking was based on God's truth, and whether your love for others demonstrated the fruit of the Spirit.

Perhaps God has convicted you of offending your brother or sister, or having false beliefs about who you really are. If you are at this point, you have realized how you have distorted the image of God by not applying biblical truth to your cultural type, but you desire to do so.

As you consider your responses to cultural differences, you may realize that you have not accepted yourself as created in God's image and how that has influenced your view of others. The restoration of God's image involves the intentional decision to forgive and be forgiven, to reconcile and to be reconciled. Most of us do not do this well culturally. Because this topic (forgiveness and reconciliation) has been described in detail in other books[37] it will not be discussed here. The point here is to spend time in prayer with God, asking Him how to forgive and how to be reconciled.

If you have never spent extended times in reflective prayer, you may want to begin by spending only 10 to 15 minutes at a time asking God for direction on the issues He brings to your mind. There are a number of books that can guide you in reflective prayer practices.[38] You can also get suggestions from someone who already practices reflective prayer.

Spend time praying and asking God what changes you need to make in order to reflect His image more clearly. God can help you examine the way you make decisions, the kind of truths you uphold, and the extent to which your interpersonal relations reflect the fruit of the Spirit and promote the unity of the body of Christ.

I trust this book will be the beginning of a new phase in your journey of faith as it was for me. May God continue to open your eyes so you will understand more fully who you are as made in God's image by helping you identify how your cultural type distorts His image and how you can apply biblical truth to cultural differences. When you are able to do this, God will give you love and acceptance for people who do things differently and you will move towards restoring His image. You will find that your attitude towards yourself will begin to change as you start to view yourself as made in God's image. This, in turn, will create sympathy and openness to others as well.

When this material and these exercises are done within a multicultural team, the potential for change in how you view each other will impact your ability to do God's kingdom work together. The exciting part will be when individuals from each culture are thriving and flourishing because they know they are made in the image of God and others are treating them as made in God's image.

∽

Exercise

...10A: How your CbJS Distorts the Image of God

1. Explain in what way(s) your cultural type distorts the image of God. Individuating, Institutionalizing, Hierarching, Interrelating — or Weak or Strong Structure and Weak or Strong Community

2. Discuss your answers with a friend to see if they agree with your responses.

～

Culture Based Judging System Question #9:

Typical Sin

Choose the statement that best describes your typical sin...[39]

___1. greed because I prefer to make my own decisions and focus on getting or doing things to take care of myself and my family and can easily appear greedy to people from other cultures.

___2. silence because I prefer to follow the rules of the system and do not easily see that the system does not take care of the people in it.

___3. pride because we prefer to be loyal to the traditions of our family/group and easily think that others are not as good as we are.

___4. envy because we prefer to distribute resources equally so that we easily notice when others have more than we do.

～

Reflection #11:

Differentiating Biblical Truth from Culture

Think back through your responses to cultural differences. What do these verses say to you about the typical sin of the cultural type (listed below) that best describes you? In addition to the typical sin listed below is a list of tendencies these culture types may exhibit. How should you address differences more biblically in your relationships with people from other cultural types.

---

a. Individuating= greed (Luke 12:15; Ephesians 5:3; Colossians 3:5; 1 John 3:17)

- Self defined by individual achievements

- Competition fosters individuality

- Complain or knock others down to enhance the self

- Avoid sharing to keep more for myself

- Little responsibility for others

---

b. Institutionalizing= silence (Romans 1:32, 2:1-4; Hebrews 13:3; Psalm 14:6)

- Self defined by following the rules

- Those persons who follow the rules are in the right: Those who do not follow the rules are in the wrong

- This type of culture may allow inequality to be built into the system

- Little or no social responsibility for others

- Little responsibility for others

c. Hierarching= pride (Psalm 101:5; Proverbs 8:13; Proverbs 16:19; James 1:9)

- Identity comes from belonging to the group and behaving according to your place in the group

- Strong in-group vs out-group acceptance

- Group pressure put on those who don't conform

- Verbal "knock downs" and gossip used to increase status

- Competition used to make the group look better

d. Interrelating= envy (Exodus 20:17; Ecclesiastes 4:4; James 3:16; 1 John 3:10)

- Identity defined by belonging to the group through sharing activities and resources

- Strong in-group vs out-group acceptance

- Group pressure put on those who don't conform

- Easily identify inequalities (envy)

- Knock down and complain to make people the same

〜

REFLECTION #12:

NEXT STEP

1. In light of your previous reflections on your intercultural relationships, what do these verses say to you about reconciliation?

    2 Corinthians 5:18; Colossians 1:20; Ephesians 2:14, 16

2. Is God asking you to reconcile with a brother or sister? If so, take time to do that. If the brother or sister is not present, share with someone what God is telling you and pray for one another.

〜

EXERCISE

...10B: Reflecting the Image of God

1. Spend time in prayer individually or corporately asking God what changes He wants you or your team to make in order to reflect His image more clearly. Ask God to examine your decision making, the truth you hold on to, and your interpersonal relationships. (You might need an extended, quiet time of prayer to process these three areas one by one.)

2. Write out what God tells you or your team about how to apply biblical truth to culture differences.

3. Share what you have learned with others.

ENDNOTES

1. "Default culture is what people learn from their parents and peers from birth."

2. Hiebert calls this "premature judgment."

3. Dye explores this point further, 469-473.

4. I'll explain this in detail in Chapter 3. Basically, a Culture-based Judging System is a mechanism that we use to justify our cultural way of doing things. It involves the interplay of our decision making, beliefs, and emotions, an expression of being created in the image of God (see Chapter 2).

5. Some readers may not have just one childhood home. They can choose the one that they remember the most.

6. I later learned that stress and cancer go hand in hand. Going through this material has increased my spiritual, emotional, and physical well-being.

7. Hoekema refers to this as "human structure and functioning."

8. Heart and mind are translated from the Greek word καρδια (*kardia*) and the Hebrew word לֵב (*lev*). The word *kardia* is defined in terms of the inner person rather than the outward physical person as "the center and source of the whole inner life with its thinking, feeling, and volition," "the faculty of thought, the thoughts themselves, of understanding, as the organ of natural and spiritual enlightenment," "of the will and its decision," and "desires of the heart."

9. Douglas uses the terms Grid and Group for her two dimensions.

10. Personal communication. November 2009. I have chosen to replace these terms with Structure and Community based on my experiences in teaching these concepts in workshops and classes.

11. Thompson, Ellis, and Wildavsky call these four types Individualism, Fatalism, Hierarchy, and Egalitarianism. Lingenfelter calls them Individualist, Bureaucratic, Hierarchical, and Egalitarian. I use the terms Individuating, Institutionalizing, Hierarching, and Interrelating to characterize the activity in each of the types.

12. "Beyond the dominant, major, or orienting ideas of individualism and freedom, Americans seemed to share very little."

13. The term "US Americans" is used in this book to distinguish Americans raised in the

United States from Latins and others who live in South America and from Canadians who live in North America. We also recognize that there are subcultures and ethnic groups within the US society who may be categorized differently (e.g., recent immigrant communities, Native American groups).

14. Certain forms of communism (under Stalin, for example).

15. See Wildavsky 1984 for an analysis of the Israelites from a Grid/Group perspective.

16. The references to Australia refer to Anglo Australia rather than the Aboriginal cultures.

17. 1 reflects Individualizing, 2 reflects Institutionalizing, 3 reflects Hierarching, 4 reflects Interrelating.

18. I later had two sons and no daughters. I didn't realize the impact this had on me as my whole life had been geared towards taking care of the men in my life. My needs came last if at all. I also discovered that this was very Asian and I was following the Confucian hierarchy in which women were always to be in submission to a male person—her father, her husband, and her oldest son and serving them first.

19. Social status may be based on an ascribed inherited role or on an achieved role.

20. This is known as an Iroquois kinship system.

21. Iroquois, Omaha, and Crow kinship systems respectively.

22. This system is called the Sudanese kinship system.

23. Although these characteristics were described about children in US American culture (Leman), they also seem to apply to other cultures as a natural consequence of childrearing.

24. The firstborn Jewish boy goes through a ceremony releasing him from service in the temple.

25. 1 reflects Individuating, 2 reflects Institutionalizing, 3 reflects Hierarching, 4 reflects Interrelating

26. "Because building a house is a cultural phenomenon, its form and organization are greatly influenced by the cultural milieu in which it belongs."Rapoport, Amos. *House Form and Culture.* Upper Saddle River, NJ: Prentice Hall, 1969, 46.

27. 1 reflects Individuating, 2 reflects Institutionalizing, 3 reflects Hierarching, 4 reflects Interrelating.

28. A small container made of wood, plastic, or metal that holds two portions of the Torah in Hebrew.

29. In Indonesia when an older person approaches a porch where younger people are sitting, the younger person will show deference by moving to a lower position. Or a chair might suddenly appear for a higher status person, while others sit on the porch. Balinese also indicate ranking by where they sit.

30. There are a number of European proverbs that say guests and fish both stink after three days.

31. 1 reflects Individuating, 2 reflects Institutionalizing, 3 reflects Hierarching, 4 reflects Interrelating

32. Such as Uzbeks—breakfast, lunch, afternoon snack, and dinner.

33. The early Greeks ate two meals a day; the Romans ate three meals a day.

34. 1 reflects Individuating, 2 reflects Institutionalizing, 3 reflects Hierarching, 4 reflects Interrelating.

35. Pete Menjares and Deborah Taylor, University Diversity Leadership Committee, Biola University, personal communication.

36. Sherwood G. Lingenfelter, personal communication.

37. E.g. Ken Sande, The Peacemaker: A Biblical Guide to Resolving Conflict. Grand Rapids, MI: Baker Books, 2004. David Augsburger. Mediation Across Cultures: Pathways and Patterns. Louisville, KY: Westminster John Knox Press, 1995.

38. Thomas Merton. *Contemplative Prayer*. Memphis, TN: Image. 1971. Richard Foster. *Prayer: Finding the Heart's True Home*. New York: Harper One, 1992.

39. The verses in the four following categories address the particular sin of the four types of cultures: 1. Individuating cultures, 2. Institutionalizing cultures, 3. Hierarching cultures, 4. Interrelating cultures.

40. 1 reflects Individuating, 2 reflects Institutionalizing, 3 reflects Hierarching, 4 reflects Interrelating.

References

Abazov. Rafis. *Culture and Customs of the Central Asian Republics.* Westport, CN: Greenwood Press, 2007.

Adler, Joseph A. *Chinese Religious Traditions.* Upper Saddle River, NJ: Prentice Hall, Inc, 2002.

Alcock, Joan. *Food in the Ancient World.* Westport, CN: Greenwood Press, 2007.

Althen, Gary. *American Ways: A Guide for Foreigners in the United States.* Yarmouth, MN: Intercultural Press, 1988.

Altman, Irwin and Martin M. Chemers. *Culture and Environment.* Monterey, CA: Brooks/Cole Publishing Company, 1980.

Altman, Irwin and Mary Gauvain. "A Cross-Cultural and Dialectic Analysis of Homes." In *Spatial Representation and Behavior Across the Life Span: Theory and Application* (Developmental Psychology Series). NY: Academic Press, Inc., 1981.

Arndt, William and F. W. Gingrich. *A Greek-English Lexicon of the New Testament.* Chicago, IL: University of Chicago Press, 1957.

Ashkenazi, Michael, and Jeanne Jacob. *Food Culture in Japan.* Westport, CN: Greenwood Press, 2003.

Atkins, Robert A. Jr. *Egalitarian Community: Ethnography and Exegesis.* Tuscaloosa, AL: University of Alabama Press, 1991.

Austin, M.R. "A Description of the Maori Marae." In *The Meaning of the Built Environment: A Nonverbal Communication Approach.* Beverly Hills, CA: Sage, 1990.

Bogumil, Connie. "Humoral Theory in Cultural Food Beliefs." *Food Resource,* NFM406, 2002, 1.

Bray, Francesca. "American Modern: the Foundation of Western Civilization," http://www.anth.ucsb.edu/faculty/bray/toilet/index.html, 2004. Accessed May 2, 2007.

Brusco, Elizabeth E. *The Reformation of Machismo: Evangelical Conversion and Gender in Colombia.* Austin, TX: University of Austin, 1995.

Burnett, David. *Unearthly Powers: A Christian Perspective on Primal and Folk Religion.* Eastbourne, England: MARC, 1988.

Carroll, Raymond. "Home." In *Cultural Misunderstandings: The French and the American*. Volk, Carol, tr. Chicago, IL: University of Chicago Press, 1987.

Clark, Donald N. *Culture and Customs of Korea*. Westport, CN: Greenwood Press, 2000.

Condon, John C. and Fathi Yousef. "Out of House and Home." In *Readings in Cross-Cultural Communication: Towards Internationalism*. Cambridge, MA: Newbury House Publishers, 1975.

Cumming, William. "Squat Toilets and Cultural Commensurability: Two Texts, Plus Three Photographs I Forgot to Take,"*Journal of Mundane Behavior,* 2000.

Douglas, Mary.

Purity and Danger: An Analysis of the concepts of Pollution and Taboo. London: Routledge and Kegan Paul, 1966.

"Cultural Bias." In *In the Active Voice*. London: Routledge & Kegan Paul, 1982.

Risk and Blame: Essays in Cultural Theory. London: Routledge. 1992.

Dye, Wayne. "Toward a Cross-Cultural Definition of Sin," In *Perspectives on the World Christian Movement: A Reader*. Pasadena, CA: William Carey Library, 2009.

Elliott, Matthew A. *Faithful Feelings: Rethinking Emotion in the New Testament*. Grand Rapids, MI: Kregel Publishers, 2006.

Escobar, Samuel. "Preface." In *One World or Many? The Impact of Globalisation on Mission*. Tiplady, Richard, ed. Pasadena, CA: William Carey Library, 2003.

Forshee, Jill. *Culture and Customs of Indonesia*. Westport, CN: Greenwood Press, 2006.

Hafizullah, Emadi. *Culture and Customs of Afghanistan*. Westport, CN: Greenwood Press, 2005.

Hakansson, Tore. "House Decoration Among South Asian Peoples." In *Shelter, Sign, and Symbol*. Oliver, Paul, ed. Woodstock, NY: Overlook Press, 1980.

Hand, E.S. Craighill Handy and Mary Kawena Pukui. *The Polynesian Family System in Kau, Hawai'i*. Honolulu, HI: Mutual Publishing, 1998.

Heine, Peter. *Food Culture in the Near East, Middle East, and North Africa*. Westport, CN: Greenwood Press, 2004.

Hersman, Lynda. *Teamwork with Diversity: Grid-Group Analysis of National Structures for International Mission Teams*. Dallas, TX: SIL.

Hiebert, Paul G.

"Cultural Differences and Communication of the Gospel."In *Perspectives on the World Christian Movement: A Reader*. Pasadena, CA: William Carey Library, 2009a.

The Gospel in Human Contexts: Anthropological Explorations for Contemporary Missions. Grand Rapids, MI: Baker Academics, 2009b.

Hoekema, Andrew. *Created in God's Image*. Grand Rapids, MI: Wm. B. Eerdmans Publishing Company, 1994.

Hugh-Jones, Christine. "Concepts of Space-Time." In *From the Milk River: Spatial and Temporal Practices in the Amazonia*. Cambridge, UK: Cambridge University Press, 1972.

Johnson, S. Lewis Jr. "God gave them up. A Study in Divine Retribution." *Biblioteca Sacra*, April 1972, 125.

Kent, Susan. "A Cross-Cultural Study of Segmentation, Architecture, and the Use of Space." In *Domestic Architecture and the Use of Space*. Cambridge: University of Cambridge Press, 1990.

Khambatta, Ismet. "Hindu Dwelling." In *Dwellings, Settlements and Traditions: Cross-Cultural Perspectives*. Bourdier, Jean-Paul and AlSayyad Nezar, eds. Lanham, MD: University Press of America, 1990.

Kiple, Kenneth F. and Kriemhild Coneè Ornelas, eds.The *Cambridge World History of Food*, Volume II, Cambridge, England: Cambridge University Press, 2000.

Kira, Alexander. *The Bathroom*. London: Viking Adult, 1975.

Lawrence, Roderick J. "House Form and Culture Re-examined." In *Housing, Dwellings, and Homes*. Chichester, UK: John Wiley, 19(2), 1987.

Leman, Kevin. *The Birth Order Book: Why You Are the Way You Are*. Old Tappan, NJ: Fleming H. Revell Company, 2nd Ed., 2009.

Lingenfelter, Sherwood.

   Leading Cross-Culturally: Covenant Relationships for Effective Christian Leadership. Grand Rapids, MI: Baker Academic, 2008.

   Transforming Culture: A Challenge for Christian Mission. Grand Rapid, MI: Baker Books, 1998.

Mack, Glenn R. and Asele Surina. *Food Culture in Russia and Central Asia*. Westport, CN: Greenwood Press, 2005.

Mason, Laura. *Food Culture in Great Britain*. Westport, CN: Greenwood Press, 2004.

Maas, James. *Power Sleep*. New York: Random House Publishers. 1999.

Mernissi, Fatima. *Beyond the Veil: Male-Female Dynamics in Modern Muslim Society*. Bloomington, IN: Indiana University Press, 1987.

Milleret, Margo. "Social Customs." *Culture and Customs of Brazil*. Vincent, Jon S., ed. Westport, CN: Greenwood Press, 2003.

Morrison, Terrie and Wayne A. Conaway. *Kiss, Bow, or Shake Hands*. Avon, MA: Adams Media, 2006.

Mosler, David. *Australia, the Recreational Society*. Westport, CN: Praeger Publishers, 2002.

Naylor, Larry L. *American Culture: Myth and Reality of a Culture of Diversity*. Westport, CN: Bergin & Garvey Paperback, 1998.

Oliver, Paul. *Dwellings*. New York: Phaidon Press, 2003.

Oseeo-Asare, Fran. *Food Culture in Sub-Suharan Africa (Food Culture Around the World)*. Westport, CN: Greenwood Press, 2005.

Pader, Ellen J. "Spatiality and Social Change: Domestic Space Use in Mexico and the United States." *American Ethnologist*, 1993, 20(1): 114-137.

Platinga, Cornelius Jr. *Not the Way It's Supposed to Be: A Breviary of Sin*. Grand Rapids, MI: Wm. B. Eerdmans Publishing Company, 1994.

Pohl, Christine D. *Making Room: Recovering Hospitality as a Christian Tradition*. Grand Rapids, MI: Wm. B. Eerdmans Publishing Company, 1999.

Rakoff, Robert M. "Ideology in Everyday Life: The Meaning of the House." *Politics and Society*, 7:85-104, 1977.

Rapoport, Amos. *House Form and Culture*. Upper Saddle River, NJ: Prentice Hall, 1969.

Saucy, Robert. "Theology of Human Nature." In *Christian Perspectives on Being Human: A Multidisciplinary Approach to Integration*. Moreland, James Porter and David M. Ciocchi, eds. Grand Rapids, MI: Baker Publishing Group, 1993.

Shakhanova, Nurila Zh. "The Yurt in the Traditional Worldview of Central Asian Nomads." In *Foundations of Empire: Archeology and Art of the Eurasian Steppes*. Gary Seaman, ed. University of Southern California: Ethnographics Press, 1992.

Smith, David I. and Barbara Carvill. *The Gift of the Stranger: Faith, Hospitality, and Foreign Language Learning*. Grand Rapids, MI: Wm. B. Eerdmans Publishing Company, 2000.

Sobania, Neal. *Culture and Customs of Kenya*. Westport, CN: Greenwood Press, 2003.

Standish, Peter, and Steven M. Bell. *Culture and Customs of Mexico*. Westport, CN: Greenwood Press, 2004.

Stein, Rod. "Scientists Finding Out What Losing Sleep Does to a Body." *Washington Post*, October 9, 2005.

Stephenson, Skye. *Understanding Spanish-Speaking South Americans*. Intercultural Press, Yarmouth, ME, 2003.

Stewart, Edward C. and Milton J. Bennett. *American Cultural Patterns: A Cross-Cultural Perspective*. Yarmouth MN: Intercultural Press, 1991.

Swartley, William M. "The Relation of Justice/Righteousness to Shalom/Eirene." *Ex Auditu*, 2006, 22:30.

Thompson, Michael, Richard Ellis, and Aaron Wildavsky. *Cultural Theory*. Boulder, CO: Westview Press, 1990.

Tjahjono, Gunawan. "Center and Duality in the Javanese Dwelling. In *Dwellings, Settlements, and Tradition: Cross-Cultural Perspective*. Bourdier, Jean-Paul and Nezar Alsayyad, eds. New York: University Press of America, 1989.

Tu, Wei-Ming "Probing the 'Three Bonds' and 'Five Relationships' in Confucian Humanism." In *Confucianism and the Family*. Slote, Walter H. and George a. DeVos. NY: State University of NY Press, 1998.

Tuan, Yi-Fu. *Topofilia: A Study of Environmental Perception, Attitudes, and Values*. NY: Columbia University, 1974.

Turner, David L. "Paul and the Ministry of Reconciliation in 2 Cor. 5:11-6:2." *Criswell Theological Review*, 1989, 4.1.

Waltner, Erland. "Shalom and Wholeness." *Brethren Life and Thought*, Vol. XXIX, Summer, 1984.

Waterson, Roxana. *The Living House: An Anthropology of Architecture in SE Asia*. Singapore: Oxford University Press, 1990.

Well, Christa. *Fierce Food: The Intrepid Diner's Guide to the Unusual, Exotic and Downright Bizarre*. New York: Plume, 2006.

White, Hugh C. *Shalom in the Old Testament*. Berea, OH: United Church Press, 1973.

Wikan, Unni. "Shame and Honor: A Contestable Pair." *MAN*, 19:635-52.

Wildavsky, Aaron. *The Nursing Father: Moses as a Political Leader*. Tuscaloosa, AL: University of Alabama Press, 1984.

Wilkins, Steve and Mark L. Sanford. *Hidden Worldviews: Eight Cultural Stories that Shape Our Lives*. Downers Grove, IL: InterVarsity Press, 2009.

Zanca, Russell. "Take! Take! Take! Host-Guest Relations and All That Food: Uzbek Hospitality Past and Present." *Anthropology of East Europe Review*, 2003, Vol 21(1), 2003.

Made in the USA
Lexington, KY
09 September 2017